The Life Of John Tillotson, Archbishop Of Canterbury

F. H.

THE
LIFE

OF THE

Moſt Reverend Father in God

JOHN TILLOTSON,

Arch-Biſhop of *Canterbury*.

Compiled from the *Minutes* of the Reverend Mr. YOUNG, late Dean of *Salisbury*. By *F. H.* M. A.

WITH

Many Curious MEMOIRS communicated by the late Right Reverend GILBERT, Lord Biſhop of *Sarum*.

LONDON:

Printed for E. CURLL at the *Dial* and *Bible* againſt St. *Dunſtan's Church* in *Fleetſtreet* ; W. TAYLOR at the *Ship* in *Pater-noſter-Row* ; and J. OSBORN at the *Oxford Arms* in *Lombard-Street*. 1717.

(Price 3 *s.* 6 *d.*)

PREFACE.

THE LIFE of Arch-Bifhop TIL-
LOTSON was begun by a Re-
verend Clergyman, with a
View of paying fome Tribute
to the Memory of One who had done fo
much Honour to the *Order*. He had Collected for this Purpofe a great Number of
Materials from printed Books and Original Papers, and by a particular Intercourfe
with the late Bifhop of *Salisbury*, feemed
to have furnifhed himfelf with Matter re-
quifite to complete his Defign. But fo it
happened, that before he had gone half the
Way in his intended Scheme, he was obliged to drop it imperfect, being called A-
broad upon fome neceffary Affairs. Thus
the Defign was interrupted, and during
his Abfence fome frefh Materials dropp'd
in, which in the Courfe of the *Life* ought
to have been mention'd near the beginning.
This is the Reafon why the Reader will
fometimes find the Series of the Story not
fo well connected as it ought to be, but

he

he muſt not impute that to want of Judgment, which was only the effect of Acci-
dent.

The Perſon to whoſe Hand the finiſh-
ing this Life fell, would have thought it
a Happineſs to have had the full Plan at
once in his Eye, and hopes he ſhould then
have given his Reader more Satisfaction
in point of Method. If this Fault may be
attoned for, in another Edition he will
have Encouragement to proceed in it with
an exact Care, and with as little Offence
to any, as a Work of this Kind can be
ſubject to. In the mean time the Publick may be aſſured, that what is here
offered is genuine, and the Materials received from unexceptionable Hands, and
every Regarder of Arch-Biſhop TILLOT-
SON's Memory is hereby importun'd to do
their endeavours to make his *Hiſtory* more
complete.

As to the Prelate himſelf, however faul-
ty his Life may appear as here written, we
are certain (human Imperfection excepted, for I cannot ſay Frailties) there was
none as He lived It.

THE

THE

CONTENTS.

The CONTENTS.

———— *The*

The CONTENTS.

The CONTENTS.

THE

THE
LIFE
OF
Arch-Bishop *Tillotson.*

The INTRODUCTION.

THOSE who have under-
taken to write the Lives of
illuftrious Men, have generally chofen for the Subject
of their Hiftory, great *Princes* or victorious *Generals,*
famous *Legiflators,* or wife *Politicians,* fuch
as have fignalized themfelves by Milita-
ry Exploits, or by their prudent Admini-
ftration of Civil Affairs. PLUTARCH, and
moft of the other Biographers of Antiquity,

B   have

have acquired an immortal Name for their
Performances of this kind, for their Lives
of Persons eminent in the active Part of
Mankind: Yet DIOGENES LAERTIUS is
no less famous for writing the History of
the speculative Part, his Lives of the *Phi-
losophers*; and amongst the Moderns, the
Memory of the Learned CAVE will live
for ever, for his incomparable History of
the Primitive Fathers. If the one of these
affords us greater Variety of Matter for
our Diversion, the other gives us a more
excellent Example for our Imitation.

Amongst the vast number of those who
have passed thro' this World, few have
done any thing worth recording for the use
of Posterity; far the greater Number have
either spent their Time in a silent Obscu-
rity, or misemployed their Activity: So
that their Bodies and their Names have
been buried together in Oblivion, or brand-
ed with a Mark of Infamy, for the warning and terrour of succeeding Ages. And
even amongst those who have made the
most glorious Figure, and acted the most
famous Part upon the Stage of this World,
many have owed their Renown to their
high Birth and Quality, to their great
Riches, or to some other external Helps
and Advantages, or some fortunate ac-
cidental Events, more than to their own
personal Merits, and internal Accomplish-
ments

ments and Endowments : Yet all Ages
have produced some few (tho' very few
indeed) who have distinguished themselves
by their extraordinary Actions, which have
given a Lustre to their Names, the Fame
of which will endure for ever. So great
have been their Abilities, that they have
conquer'd all the Difficulties, and sur-
mounted all the Obstacles, which their
most inveterate and implacable Enemies
have raised against them. So inimitable
have been their Lives, and such great Bleffings have they proved to the World, that
even Envy and Malice have not been able
to detract from them, but they have shone
the brighter thro' the thickest of those
Clouds which have been raised to obscure
them. Amongst which Number may justly be ranked this Great and Good Man,
whose Life I will endeavour to write. He
was neither of noble Birth, nor had he
a great Estate, or any other external Advantage whatever, to recommend him;
but his Rise was owing entirely to his
real Worth and Goodness. His Soul was
too great for an useless unactive Life, and
his Piety and Integrity too conspicuous for
him to be justly charged with abusing his
uncommon Abilities, or misemploying his
considerable Interest. He laboured under
as many Difficulties as most Men, and yet
his extraordinary Merit advanced his Re-

putation

putation to that height, that it will out-live the Calumnies of all his Detractors.

It is a furprizing thing, that even Im-pudence and Malice fhould dare to attack fo great a Name; who fhone fo glorioufly in the univerfal Admiration of the Age in which he lived, and whofe Lofs put both Church and State under the deepeft Mourn-ing : Yet, alas ! neither the profoundeft Learning, nor the ftricteft Vertue, and moft exalted Piety, is Antidote ftrong e-nough to expel the Poifon of Mens Tongues. Even this bleffed Saint was not only perfe-cuted by the Malice of abfurd and wicked Men whilft he was alive, but were it pof-fible, they would difturb him in his Grave ; but his Fame as well as his Perfon are a-bove their Malice. One would think the leaft that can be expected, is, that he fhould be treated with Humanity, if not with Refpect ; fince he was the greateft Example that ever was known of a Gentle-nefs that could not be furprized nor over-come ; and was free from ufing any of thofe Liberties in fpeaking of others, which in fo boundlefs a meafure were taken a-gainft himfelf. It is a common Practice with Perfons who have not Abilities fuf-ficient to perform any Work by which they may become known to the World, to en-deavour at a Name and Character, by raking in the Afhes, and blackening the

Repu-

Reputation of Men of real Worth, Piety, and Learning. This eminent Prelate has been afperfed, and fuffered fufficiently in this kind. One has taken the Freedom to call him a *Socinian*, another a *Trifler* and a Denier of eternal Punifhments in another World. The Author of a Pamphlet, entituled, *Some Difcourfes upon* Dr. BURNET *and* Dr. TILLOTSON, *occafioned by the late Funeral Sermon of the former upon the latter*, has the Affurance to call him a Man who never fuffered, nor loved Sufferings; but who on the contrary was of a Temper and Conftitution that loved Eafe and Indolency; that he was not an Example of heroick Piety and Virtue; that his Life was not free from Blemifhes, and fome great ones too. And fpeaking of Dr. LEIGHTON, he fays that he was an Ufurper of the See of *Glafcow*, as Dr. TILLOTSON was efteemed in a more offenfive degree of the See of *Canterbury*. In another place he calls him a Perfon of great and dangerous Example both to the prefent Times, and to Pofterity; and fays, that he was an Atheift as much as a Man could be, tho' the graveft that ever was, and an Apoftate. " His whole Practice " (fays he) fince the Revolution, has been " one Series of Apoftacy, and by which " he hath not only difhonoured his Me" mory, and made all his other Good be

B 3 " evil

" evil fpoken of, but been a Scandal to
" our holy Church and Religion, given
" the Enemies of them great occafion to
" triumph, their beft and moft ftedfaft
" Friends great occafion of Grief and
" Shame ; and laftly, tempted loofe and
" unprincipled Men to turn Atheifts, and
" ridicule our Priefthood and Religion.
Again, he fays, " that King CHARLES
" plainly perceived that he was not quite
" freed from the Prejudices of his firft Edu-
" cation ; for when he officiated in the
" Clofet, inftead of bowing at the Name
" of *Jefus*, or rather to *Jefus* at the men-
" tioning of his Saviour's Name, that he
" might feem to do fomething, and yet
" not do the thing it felf; he ufed to ftep
" and bend backward, cafting up his Eyes
" to Heaven : which the King obferving,
" faid, he bowed the wrong way, as the
" *Quakers* do, when they falute their
" Friends : and that tho' his Majefty, who
" was a great Difcerner of Men, perfectly
" knew him, he preferred him to gratify
" the Heads of a Party : and may all Prin-
" ces, who for politick Ends prefer thofe
" for whom they have no true Kindnefs,
" and who have no true Kindnefs for
" them, be requited as he was. Another
calls him a *thorough-paced Phanatic* ; and
there was a *Memorandum* found in the
Study of the Reverend Mr. CREECH,

which

which exceedingly reflects upon this most Excellent Arch-Bishop, which I had from a very good Hand, and which I think ought to be taken notice of. It is as follows : " *Memorandum*, That whatever " Steps were taken, and all that was " done, for the abolishing Episcopacy, and " Subverfion of the Church of *Scotland*, " was done by the Contrivance, Advice, " and Approbation of Dr. TILLOTSON. And then he adds, " This I had from " JOHNSON, who was certain of it, and " knew the whole Matter, when I was " down in the North. Mankind is indeed too much difpofed to receive Defamation, from what Hand foever it comes; and no fort of it is fo welcome, as when the Clergy defame one another : Yet when it is managed with fo particular a Virulence of Style, and Blacknefs of Malice, it grows too fulfome and odious, few can bear it : Few believe a Man, who fhews too much Heat, to be fincere and candid : it really turns back upon thofe who ufe it ; the World will think the worfe of Men, when they feem to be frantick with Rage. This Spirit has fuch ugly Chara&ters, that how much foever Men may be pleafed at firft reading with the Sarcafms of Libels, yet they muft be a little better dreffed up, and not delivered in fo romantick a Strain, before they can gain credit. And

B 4   indeed

indeed the Antagonifts of this immortal
Man have not Art enough to difguife their
Malice, nor Skill enough to give their
Falfhoods the Colours, not to fay of Truth,
but even of Probability.

To violate the Quiet of the Dead, and
purfue the Afhes of Men, who have finifh-
ed their Courfe, and cannot anfwer for
themfelves, would pafs for a Crime againft
Nature, even amongft the moft barbarous
Nations : But the blackeft Spleen, and the
moft refined Malice cannot difturb this
bleffed Soul, who is enter'd into his Reft,
nor fignify much to leffen the Veneration
that all future Generations will pay his
Memory. He is now above Envy, and
beyond Slander, and his Name is and will
be long remembred with Honour, when
it will not be fo much as known, that the
greateft of his Enemies was ever born.

Among the many Misfortunes which
our unhappy Divifions have brought upon
us, it is not the leaft, that a good Man in
an eminent Station fuffers in his Reputation, from thofe who efpoufe a Party contrary to that which he is reported to be of;
and cannot obtain that univerfal good Character, which his Merit would claim, in
a Nation that is at Unity with it felf.
Thofe that were his Enemies in his Life-
time, will fall upon an Author that fhall
undertake to do him Juftice after his Death.

But

But I hope the Memory of the worthy Prelate, whofe LIFE I have undertaken, is fo dear to all good Chriftians, efpecially to the Members of the Church of *England*, that I fhall run no hazard of difpleafing any Side, unlefs it be through the Meannefs of my Performance, in not coming up to the Praifes which this Excellent Arch-Bifhop juftly deferved; and that is more my Misfortune than my Fault.

Thofe that are apprehenfive of the greateft Dangers from *Popery*, have as much reafon to hold his Memory dear, as thofe that fear the *Church* fhould be fhaken by the SCHISM of our Diffenters: for with foft Words and ftrong Arguments he reafoned away the Superftitions of the Idolaters of *Rome*, and with the Warmth of his Charity melted the ftubborn Hearts of feveral *Non-Conformifts* of his own Country.

I muft own that a Confcioufnefs of my Incapacity might have diffuaded me from entering upon fo difficult a Work with the few Materials I could get: yet I rather chofe to be taxed with giving an imperfect, tho' true Account, than wrong the Public of what I knew of the LIFE of that pious Man, whofe WORKS have been fo well received, and whofe Name will never be forgotten.

JOHN

His Birth and Education. JOHN TILLOTSON was the Son of ROBERT TILLOTSON, of *Sowerby* in the County of *Tork,* a Clothier, by MARY the Daughter of THOMAS DOPSON of *Sowerby,* Gentleman, in the Parish of *Halifax :* He was there born either the latter End of *September,* or the Beginning of *October,* in the Year One Thousand Six Hundred and Thirty. Now there having been a scandalous Story raised of this Great and Good Man in King CHARLES the Second's Time, and since revived with more Virulency upon his last Preferment, to which he was so justly promoted, *That we had a Father of our Church, who was never a Son of it ;* some of his Friends (it was, as I have been informed, the Marquis of *Halifax,* his constant Patron and Friend) to stop the Mouth of Slanderers, made application to the Minister and Church-Wardens of *Halifax,* about searching their Register, of which they transmitted the following Certificate, which is not judged improper to be here inserted.

THESE *are to certify, that* JOHN TILLOTSON, *the Son of* ROBERT TILLOTSON, *of* Sowerby *in the Parish of* Halifax, *and County of* York, *was baptized at* Halifax *aforesaid the third Day of* October, *in the Year of our Lord One Thousand Six Hundred*

Hundred and Thirty; *as appears by our Pa-*
rish Register.

Ita Teft. { Jos. WILKINSON, Vicar.
de Halifax.
Jo. GAUKROGER, Cler.
Paroch. de Halifax.

So great Veneration they bear to the Memory of that good Man, that not content
with this Certificate, they, upon his De-
cease, were pleafed to put up this Infcrip-
tion in Letters of Gold in the Church of
Halifax.

JOHANNES TILLOTSON, *Archiepifcopus*
Cantuarienfis, natus Sowerbiæ, renatus
Halifaxiæ 3tio Octobris, 1630. *dena-*
tus Lambethæ 22do Novembris, A. D.
1694. *Ætatis* 65. i. e.

JOHN TILLOTSON, Arch-Bifhop
of *Canterbury,* was born at *Sowerby,* baptized at *Halifax* the third of *October,*
1630. and died at *Lambeth* the twenty fecond of *November,* One Thoufand Six Hundred and Ninety Four, in the fixty fifth
Year of his Age.

His firft Education and Impreffions
were among thofe who were then called
Puritans, but of the beft fort : Yet even
before his Mind was opened to clearer
Thoughts, he felt fomewhat within him,
that

that difpofed him to larger Notions, and a better Temper. The Books which were put into the Hands of the Youth of that Time, were generally heavy; he could fcarce bear them, even before he knew better things: He happily fell on CHIL- LINGWORTH's Book, which gave his Mind the Ply that it held ever after, and put him on a true Scent. He was foon freed from his firft Prejudices, or rather, he was never maftered by them: Yet he ftill ftuck to the Strictnefs of Life to which he was bred, and retained a juft Value and a due Tendernefs for the Men of that Perfuafion; and by the Strength of his Reafon, toge- ther with the Clearnefs of his Principles, he brought over more ferious Men from their Scruples to the Communion of the Church, and fix'd more in it, than any Man I ever knew *.

He is ad- mitted in the Uni- verfity. After he had with a quick Proficiency gone through the Grammar-Schools, and arrived to an uncommon Knowledge in the learned Languages, he was on *April* the twenty third, in the Year One Thou- fand Six Hundred and Forty Seven, ad- mitted Penfioner of *Clare-Hall* in *Cam- bridge*, under the Tuition of Mr. *David Clarkfon*: He commenced Batchelor of

---

* his Funeral Sermon.

Arts

Arts at *Midsummer* One Thousand Six Hundred and Fifty, and was elected Fellow before *Christmas* that Year. In Sixteen Hundred and Fifty Four he took the Degree of Master of Arts, and in Sixty Six went out Doctor in Divinity. There have been a Load of Calumnies cast upon him relating to his Conduct during his Residence in *Clare-Hall* ; I shall set them down in the Words of the Author of the Pamphlet already mentioned *, and then I will plainly make appear the Falsity of them. His Words are as follow.

" Not long after he came thither (to
" *Cambridge)* King CHARLES the First
" was brought by *Cambridge* to *Hampton-*
" *Court,* and lodging at Sir *John Cuts* his
" House at *Childerly* near that University,
" the Scholars went thither to kiss his
" Hand : but he, and some few more, had
" so signalized themselves for those they
" then called *Round-heads,* that they were
" not admitted to that Honour with the
" rest of the Scholars. Within a Year or
" two after he went out Midsummer Bat-
" chelor of Arts; by which having local-
" ly qualified himself for a Fellowship, he
" got the Rump's *Mandamus* for Dr. *Gun-*
" *ning's* (which I think one of his own

---

* *Some Discourses on Dr.* Burnet, *and Dr.* Tillotson, &c.

" Gang

" Gang enjoyed a little before him) as a
" Reward for his good Affection to the
" Cause. From that time to his difconti-
" nuance he governed the College, the
" Senior Fellows not daring to oppofe him,
" becaufe of the Intereft he had with his
" great Mafters ; and fo zealous was he
" for them, that the Corner of the Col-
" lege, which he and his Pupils took up
" in the New Building, was called the
" *Round-head Corner.* And when King
" CHARLES the Second was beaten at
" *Worcefter,* he fent for the Tables, in
" which the College Grace was written,
" and after the Paffage of Thankfgiving
" for their Benefactors, *Te laudamus pro*
" *benefactoribus noftris, &c.* he added with
" his own Hand, and of his own Head,
" *præfertim pro nuperâ victoriâ contra* CA-
" ROLUM STUARTUM *in agro Wigornienfi*
" *reportatâ,* or to that effect. In the Year
" 1656, or in the Beginning of 1657, he
" difcontinued from the College, being in-
" vited by PRIDEAUX, CROMWELL's At-
" torney General, to teach his Son, and
" do the Office of a Chaplain in his Fa-
" mily.

To thefe falfe and groundlefs Afperfions
I fhall anfwer in the Words of two very
Learned Perfons. The firft is the Right
Reverend the late Lord Bifhop of *Sarum,* in
his Reflections upon the forefaid Pamphlet,
" There

" There is (ſays he) *Page 62, 63.* a long Reflecti-
" Account given of many Particulars re- ons, *p.*
" lating to the Arch-Biſhop during his 164, 165,
" Stay at *Clare-Hall*; upon which a very 166.
" worthy Member of that Body has told
" me, that they have been enquiring into
" the Truth of theſe, and that they find
" them to be falſe. He was admitted to
" that Houſe *April* 23d, 1647. It was no
" wonder if ſuch a Freſh-man was not
" admitted to the Honour of kiſſing the
" King's Hand, when he was in that
" Neighbourhood two Months after that :
" It is not likely that he pretended to it;
" or that it would have been denied, if he
" had. He was Batchelor of Arts, *Mid-*
" *ſummer*, 1650. and became a Fellow be-
" fore *Chriſtmas* that Year. Dr. GUN-
" NING had been turned out ſix Years be-
" fore that ; ſo that it cannot be ſaid he
" came into his Fellowſhip. Men may
" conſider the Avoidance that did imme-
" diately go before their Admiſſion ; but
" I never heard of any who were ſo ſcru-
" pulous as to run the Enquiry farther.
" As for the taking on him to alter the
" Grace after Meat, and to add a ſpecial
" Mention of *Worceſter* Fight ; there is
" no Memory of any ſuch thing that ever
" happened in that Houſe : It is not likely
" that a Junior Fellow, and ſo young a
" Batchelor of Arts, could have preſumed
" to

" to have done such a thing, or that the
" *Master* and Senior Fellows could have
" suffered it. Dr. BLYTHE, the pre-
" sent *Master*, and Dr. VINCENT, the
" Senior Fellow of the House, were
" admitted soon after that ; but never
" heard of any thing of that nature.
" Every one that knows those Bodies,
" will easily believe that such things are
" not soon forgot in them. In the Year
" 1660, as is ordinary upon such Revolu-
" tions, all Stories of that sort were re-
" membred, and Characters were made
" of Men accordingly ; but this was not
" then spoke of, and after an Oblivion of
" 45 Years, a Knight of the Post at last is
" found, who affirms it : but I believe
" few give any Credit to it. These two
" Reverend Persons do likewise affirm,
" that the late Arch-Bishop was, as long
" as they can remember him, the modest
" and good-natured Man that we all knew
" him to be in a higher Elevation.

The other Account of the Arch-Bishop's
Behaviour while he was in the College,
was sent by Mr. DENTON, a very worthy
Member of *Clare-Hall*, to his Friend,
which I shall here insert *verbatim*, as it
was communicated by the Reverend
Mr. WHISTON.

SIR,

SIR,

I Have thus long deferr'd to return an Answer to your Letter about the late very worthy *Arch-Bishop* of Canterbury, because I was desirous to give you as punctual an Account as I could of those things laid to his charge in the *Libel*. I have found out two Persons who, besides my self, were in Clare-Hall *that Summer in which* Worcester *Fight was*, viz. Sir WATKINSON PAYLER, *who was Nobleman*, and Mr. JA. MOUNTAIN, *who was Fellow of the College*; *and if there had been any such* Alteration *made by him in the College Grace, as the* Pamphlet *mentions, surely some of us who daily heard it read, would have known it*; *but those Persons do profess, as I do, they never knew nor heard of any such thing done or attempted to be done, but do believe it to be a malicious Lie. I perceive I was mistaken in the Time of his being made Fellow, which (you say) by the* Buttery Books *appears to be some time before* Worcester *Fight, and I must believe that Record before my Memory at this distance of Time. I was also in the College when King* CHARLES I. *pass'd by* Cambridge, *and whether* TILLOTSON *went to* Sir JONH CUTTS's *House, amongst several that did, I have forgotten*; *but I am pretty confident the Story of his being denied the Honour to kiss his Majesty's Hand, is not*

C   *true*;

true ; *for I never heard of any such thing,
which (if it had been so) I should certainly
have done, if not from him, from some others,
several of my Acquaintance being there.* It
is true that he had Dr. GUNNING's *Fellowship, but whether by a* Mandamus, *or
the College Election, I cannot certainly tell,
but believe the latter : for when he came into it, it was made void by the Death of
one who had enjoyed it several Years after*
Dr. GUNNING *left it ; and I think none of
those Fellowships were filled, after the first
turn, by* Mandamus's; *but of this I am not
certain, and forgot to ask Mr.* MOUNTAIN
*about it, when I was with him, who pro-
bably may remember that better than I ; but
I will, as soon as I have an Opportunity,
speak or write to him about it. As for
what the* Pamphlet *says of his governing the
College, the Senior Fellows not daring to op-
pose, because of the Interest he had with his
great Masters, it is very malicious and false ;
for he was not of an imperious Humour, but
had then that Sweetness of Temper which
he ever after retain'd, and was much re-
spected by the Senior Fellows. He was indeed in those young Years of very great Parts
and Prudence, and the Senior Fellows would
always have his Advice in what was done
about College-Affairs, giving that great De-
ference to his Judgment. And Mr.* MOUN-
TAIN *(who was one of the Senior Fellows,*
and

and as much as any one for the King's side,
having been some Years in his Army) does to
this day retain a very great Honour for him,
and never mentions him without a mighty
Respect.

Some time before the Reſtauration of
King CHARLES the Second, he was made
Curate to Biſhop WILKINS in St. LAW-
RENCE's Church in the City of *London*;
with whom the Biſhop was ſo well ſatiſ-
fied, that he declared he had been a great
while ſeeking for one to pleaſe him, and
now had found him. And at his Death
he was pleaſed by his laſt Will to commit
all his Papers to his Care, and out of his
great Friendſhip, left them wholly to his
diſpoſal, out of which, in the Year One
Thouſand Six Hundred and Seventy Five,
he publiſhed that learned Treatiſe of the
Principles and Duties of Natural Religion,
in two Books, with a Prefatory Diſcourſe,
giving an account of the Work, which
ſhall be inſerted in its proper Place.

In the Years Sixteen Hundred and Sixty
One and Two he was Curate to Dr. HAC-
KET, Vicar of *Cheſhunt* in *Hartfordſhire*,
as abundance of the Pariſhioners living
there did well remember; particularly
Mr. MOTT the Pariſh-Clark and School-
maſter, who gave the following Account
of him, *viz.* That Sir THOMAS DACRES

Made Cu-
rate to Dr.
Wilkins.

Made Cu-
rate to Dr.
Hacket.

C 2　　　　　gave

gave him his Board, who then lived at the great House near the Church; that he behaved himself there exceeding well, and did a great many good things; amongst the rest, by his mild and gentle Behaviour, and perfuasive Eloquence, he prevailed with an old *Oliverian* Soldier, who set up for an Anabaptist Preacher there, and preached in a red Coat, and was much followed in that Place, to defift from that Encroachment upon the Parish Minister, and the Ufurpation of the Priest's Office, and to betake himself to some honeft Employment. He alfo married a Couple who had lately had a Baftard Child betwixt them; he gave them a decent but fevere Reprimand for their former Wickedness, together with a ferious Exhortation to a holy Life. Some Years after he and Dr. *Stillingfleet* hired the great House beforementioned, and lived there together in the Summer time.

Prefented to the Rectory of Ketton, alias Keddington.

It has been confidently reported, that he never had a Cure of Souls; but in *Butteley's* Edition of *Somner's Antiquities of Canterbury,* Part 3. p. 124. it appears that he was prefented by Sir Thomas Barnadiston to the Rectory of *Ketton,* alias *Keddington,* in the County of *Suffolk:* his Mandate of Induction is there fet down *verbatim,* as it is enter'd in the Register of the Arch-Deacon of *Sudbury,* and is as follows.

follows. *Anno* 1663. *Jun.* 18. *emanavit Mandatum ad inducendum* JOHANNEM TIL-LOTSONUM, *Artium Magiſtrum, in Rectoriam de Ketton, alias Keddington, per non ſubſcriptionem (ſecundum Actum Parliamenti in eo caſu proviſum)* SAMUELIS FAIR-CLOUGH *(qui inductus fuerat anno* 1629.) *ultimi incumbentis jam ibidem vacantem.* Regiſt. *induct. Archidiac. Sudbury* ; i. e, In the Year 1663, *June* 18th, was iſſued out a Mandate to induct JOHN TIL-LOTSON, Maſter of Arts, into the Rectory of *Ketton,* alias *Keddington,* which is now there vacant by the Non-ſubſcription (as it is in that caſe provided by Act of Parliament) of SAMUEL FAIRCLOUGH, who was inducted in the Year 1629. He was inſtalled Canon of this Church, 1669, and upon the Death of Dean TURNER, 1672. was from his Canonry promoted to the Deanery of this Church. He was a moſt celebrated Preacher, as the Chapel of *Lincolns-Inn,* and the Pariſh-Church of St. *Lawrence Jury,* where he lies interred, can ſufficiently witneſs. Thus far BAT-TELEY. He did not continue there a full Year, but removed again to *London,* and procured *Keddington* to be beſtowed upon his Curate : " A Benefice (ſays the Bi-" ſhop of *Sarum* in his Funeral Sermon) " being offered him in the Country, he " once intended to have left this great

C 3   "Scene

" Scene, and gone to that Retirement,
" where he spent almost a Year; but he
" was happily recalled by that honourable
" Society (*Lincolns-Inn*) for whom he al-
" ways retain'd just Impressions of Grati-
" tude. And tho' in the Intervals of
" Terms he could have given a large Part
" of the Year to his Parish, yet so strict
" he was to the Pastoral Care in the Point
" of Residence, that he parted with it
" even when his Incomes here could scarce
" support him.

Chosen Preacher to Lin-colns-Inn.
In the Year Sixteen Hundred and Sixty Four he was chosen Preacher to *Lincolns-Inn,* where he continued some Years, and was wonderfully admired and loved by that Honourable and Learned Society, for his eloquent Sermons. Whilst he was Preacher there, he is charged with giving the Sacrament of the Lord's Supper to those who would receive it in no Posture, but that irreverent one of sitting. " A great
" Lady (says my Author *) of Dr. Owen's
" Congregation, and one of his Hearers
" too, would sometimes resort thither to
" receive the Sacrament, because, as she
" told a Noble Lord of my Acquaint-
" ance, she could receive it there sitting.

---

* *Some Discourses upon Dr.* Burnet *and Dr.* Tillotson, *occasioned by the late Funeral Sermon of the former upon the latter.*

" And

" And his Practice (as a devout Gentle-
" woman, who lived in that Neighbour-
" hood, assured me) was first to walk a-
" bout with the Elements to those in the
" Pews, where the Sitters were, and
" give it them first; but in the last place
" to those who kneeled at the Rail, with-
" in which he would not go, as Decency
" would have directed another Man, but
" coming behind them, he gave it to them
" in the Letter of the Proverb, *over the*
" *Left Shoulder.* He goes on and says,
" I could give other Instances of this na-
" ture in the other Sacrament of Baptism,
" wherein the defunct Hero hath acted
" without excuse against the Church's
" Orders, to the great Scandal of others
" who came to know it, in the violating
" the prescribed Rules of Decency and
" Edification. The Truth of this Story
has been carefully enquired into, but there
does not appear the least ground to believe
it. There is not one living Witness of it,
nor any Record (but our Author's) nor so
much as any oral Tradition for it; but by
the most authentick Accounts that can be
had, this worthy Person, during his Abode
in that Learned Society, did observe the
greatest Decency in administring in holy
things, and was strictly conformable to
the Rules and Orders of the Church of
England. But granting the Report to be
true,

true, no temperate Perſon can eſteem it a Crime of ſo deep a Dye, as the Author of it repreſents it to be; for the Poſture in which the Sacrament of the Lord's Supper was at firſt adminiſtred, was no part of the Inſtitution; ſo that the Inſtitution is not broken, in what Poſture ſoever it is received. Kneeling (tho' undoubtedly it is the moſt reverent, and moſt becoming this holy and venerable Ordinance) nor any other Poſture, has any Command at all for it : So that no particular Poſture is abſolutely neceſſary, but all are left indifferent, and may lawfully be uſed, either as publick Authority, or in want thereof, as private Prudence and Love of Peace ſhall determine us.

Choſen Le-
Ʊurer at
St. Law-
rence's
Church in
London.

The ſame Year he was choſen Tueſday-Lecturer of St. *Lawrence's* Church in *London.* Here it was that he preached thoſe incomparable Sermons concerning the Divinity and Incarnation of our Bleſſed Saviour, in vindication of himſelf from the Calumny of Socinianiſm, with which his Enemies charged him. " When the Party (ſays " the late Learned Biſhop of *Sarum* ‖) had " given credit to a moſt impudent Calum-" ny that was raiſed by the Papiſts againſt " the late Primate, of his being a Soci-

---

‖ *Reflections upon a Pamphlet, entituled,* Some Diſcourſes upon Dr. *Burnet* and Dr. *Tillotſon, &c.*

" *nian,*

" *nian*, his Book againſt thoſe Errors had
" for ſome time made even the Party
" it ſelf aſhamed to ſupport that any
" longer; at laſt an ignorant and mali-
" cious Writer * was found out to main-
" tain that Charge ſtill, which had made
" too great a Noiſe to be eaſily parted
" with. But I am heartily glad to ſee
" Juſtice done to the Name of ſo great a
" Man, by one † who has anſwered that
" Libel in ſo full and ſo convincing a man-
" ner. He has concealed no Part of their
" Objections; and by ſetting down all
" thoſe Parts of the Arch-Biſhop's Ser-
" mons, upon which theſe Men have ſtu-
" died to fix their Malice, not only in
" ſome ſhort Periods, which malicious
" Men have made a Noiſe with, but in
" all that went before and after, he gives
" ſo fair as well as true a Repreſentation
" of that Great Prelate's Senſe, that I am
" confident no ill Impreſſions will ſtick
" with any who will be ſo juſt as to con-
" ſider the whole Matter, the Vindication
" as well as the Calumnies, with ſincere
" and equitable Minds. The Author of
the Life of Mr. THOMAS FIRMIN, who
was a grand Socinian himſelf, has ſo fully

---

* *A Book entituled*, Conſiderations on the Explications
of the Doctrine of the Trinity.
† Dr. William's *Vindication of the Sermons of his Grace*
John *Arch-Biſhop of* Canterbury, &c.

cleared the Arch-Biſhop from that Imputation, and proved that he liv'd and died
of a contrary Opinion, that I hope it will
not be unacceptable to the Reader to inſert
the Place at large.   " Now alſo he (Mr.
" Firmin) grew into Intimacy with Dr.
" Whichcot, Dr. Worthington, Dr.
" Wilkins, Mr. Tillotson.   Dr. Wil-
" kins was afterward Biſhop of *Cheſter*,
" Mr. Tillotson (for he was not yet
" made Doctor) Arch-Biſhop of *Canter-*
" *bury :* But in their Dignity, and to the
" very laſt, Mr. Firmin had the ſame
" place and degree in their Eſteem and
" Friendſhip, that at any time formerly he
" had.   While Dr. Tillotson preached
" the Tueſday's Lecture at St. *Lawrence's,*
" ſo much frequented by all the Divines
" of the Town, and by a great many Per-
" ſons of Quality and Diſtinction ; when
" the Dr. was obliged to be at *Can-*
" *terbury*, where he was Dean, or was
" out of Town, either for Diverſion or
" Health ; he generally left it to Mr. Fir-
" min to provide Preachers for his Lecture,
" and Mr. Firmin never failed to ſupply
" his Place with ſome very eminent
" Preacher ; ſo that there never was any
" Complaint on the account of Dr. Til-
" lotson's Abſence.   And this Mr. Fir-
" min could eaſily do ; for now there was
" hardly a Divine of Note (whether in
" *London,*

" *London*, or in the Country, that fre-
" quented *London*) but Mr. FIRMIN was
" come acquainted with him. Which
" thing helped him much to serve the In-
" terefts of many hopeful young Preachers
" and Scholars, Candidates for Lectures,
" Schools, Cures, or Rectories; for whom
" he would folicit with as much Affection
" and Diligence, as other Men do for their
" Sons, or near Relations. Her late Ma-
" jefty (Queen MARY) of moft Happy
" Memory, having heard much of Mr.
" FIRMIN's Ufefulnefs in all publick De-
" figns, efpecially thofe of Charity; and
" that he was Heterodox in the Articles
" of the Trinity, the Divinity of our Sa-
" viour, and the Satisfaction; fhe fpoke
" to Arch-Bifhop TILLOTSON, and ear-
" neftly recommended it to him to fet
" Mr. FIRMIN right in thofe weighty and
" neceffary Points. The Arch-Bifhop an-
" fwered, that he had often endeavoured
" it; but Mr. FIRMIN having fo early
" and long imbibed the Socinian Doctrine,
" was not now capable of a contrary Im-
" preffion. However his Grace publifhed
" his Sermons (formerly preached at St.
" *Lawrence*'s) concerning thofe Queftions,
" and fent Mr. FIRMIN one of the firft
" Copies from the Prefs. Mr. FIRMIN
" not convinced by his Grace's Reafon-
" ings, or his Arguments from holy Scripture,

" ture, caufed a refpectful Anfwer (al-
" tho' fome have ftretched one Expreffi-
" on too far) entituled, *Confiderations on*
" *the Explications and Defences of the*
" *Doctrines of the Trinity*, to be drawn
" up and publifhed, himfelf giving his
" Grace a Copy of it. I muft not omit
" to do the Arch-Bifhop right againft thofe
" who pretend, that the Arch-Bifhop,
" notwithftanding thofe Sermons, was
" in his Heart an *Unitarian*. For Mr.
" FIRMIN himfelf told me, fhortly after
" the Arch-Bifhop had publifhed thofe
" Sermons, that going to *Lambeth*, and
" the Arch-Bifhop happening to dine in
" Private, he fent for Mr. FIRMIN to
" him, and faid to this Effect, that the
" Calumnies of the People had obliged
" him to publifh his Sermons, fome time
" fince preached at St. *Lawrence*'s againft
" the Tenents of SOCINUS : That he had
" fincerely preached, as he then thought,
" and continued ftill to think of thofe
" Points : That however no Body's falfe
" Imputations fhould provoke him to
" give ill Language to Perfons who dif-
" fented confcientioufly, and for weigh-
" ty Reafons, that he knew well this
" was the Cafe of the *Socinians*, for whofe
" Learning and Dexterity, he fhould
" always have a refpect, as well as for
" their Sincerity and Exemplarinefs. Af-
" terwards

" terwards, when Mr. FIRMIN gave him
" a Copy of the *Considerations:* After he
" had read it, he only said, *My Lord of Sa-*
" *rum shall humble their Writers.* Nor did
" he afterwards at any Time express the
" least coldness on the account of the An-
" swer made to him, but used Mr. FIR-
" MIN as formerly, enquiring as his custom
" was, *How does my Son* GILES? So he cal-
" led Mr. FIRMIN's Son by his second
" Wife. In his Funeral Sermon, we
have the following Account of his preaching this Lecture. " I need not tell you
" (says the Eloquent Preacher) how ma-
" ny Years, and with what Labour and
" Success he divided himself between
" that Society (*Lincolns-Inn*) and this
" Place. I am confident you have profi-
" ted so much by it, that you will re-
" member it long: And that you do rec-
" kon it as a great Item of the Account
" you must all one Day give, that you
" were so long blessed with his Ministry.
" The numerous Assembly that this Le-
" cture brought together, even from the
" remotest Parts of this wide City; the
" great Concourse of Clergy-men, who
" came hither to form their Minds, the
" happy Union that thereby the Clergy
" of this great Body grew into, and the
" blessed Effects this had, are Things
" which it is to be hoped an Age will not
                          " wear

" wear out of Mens Minds. Some great
" Charity, some public Service, or good
" Design was the work of most of those
" Days. Every one saw him considered
" as the Head of this learned and emi-
" nent Body: As he was the only Per-
" son that made no Reflections on it him-
" self: He was still so affable and hum-
" ble, so modest, and so ready to serve
" the youngest and meanest in it, that
" such as saw all that, must needs feel
" the Impressions of it go deep, and stick
" long with him.

He gets o-
ther Pre-
ferments. In 1669. he was made Canon of *Christ's*
Church in *Canterbury*, and Prebend of St.
Paul's in 1675, he was also preferred to
the Deanery of *Norwich*, thence to the
Deanery of *Canterbury* in 1672. and in
1689. he was made Residentiary of St.
Paul's, and Clerk of the Closet to King
WILLIAM the Third, and upon the Promotion of Dr. STILLINGFLEET from the
Deanery of St. *Paul's* to the Bishoprick
of *Worcester*, he succeeded him, all the
same Year.

Has a Con-
ference
with Mr. In 1674. King CHARLES the second,
Baxter a- who had an Apprehension and Judgment
bout a Bill (when he applied to Business) equal to
of Compre- the greatest of his Predecessors, did clear-
hension. ly perceive it to be the Sense of his Council, and the Voice of his People, that he
should Support the Established Church,
         with

with a ſtrict Hand upon the *Papiſts*, and
with a moderate reſtraint of the *Diſſen-*
ters, chiefly becauſe their Diviſion gave
Advantage to the other Enemy. On this
Principle of Wiſdom, his Majeſty commanded his own Inclination, and during
the long receſs of Parliament, to quiet
the Minds of his People, he publiſhed this
Declaration for enforcing a late Order
made in Council.

The King's Declaration.

CHARLES R.

" THE Adminiſtration of Juſtice, ac-
" cording to the ſettled and known
" Laws of our Kingdom, we take to be
" the moſt reaſonable and proper Me-
" thod for attaining and preſerving the
" Peace and Safety both of Church and
" State. As therefore we find it neceſſa-
" ry, that the Laws ſhould be put in Ex-
" ecution with more Care and Diligence
" than of late they have been, ſo alſo we
" think it expedient, that the Orders we
" have already given for that purpoſe,
" ſhould be made Publick in ſuch a man-
" ner that all Men may find themſelves
" obliged to take notice of the ſame, and
" to give a due Obedience thereunto. For
" which Reaſon we have thought fit to
" declare, and do hereby publiſh and de-
" clare

" clare our Royal Will and Pleafure, that
" our Order made in Council on *Wednef-*
" *day* the Third Day of this inftant *Fe-*
" *bruary,* and fince printed and publifh-
" ed, be exactly obferved, by all and eve-
" ry Perfon and Perfons to whom it fhall
" or may appertain: And more particu-
" larly we require and command, that the
" Convictions of *Popifh* Recufants be eve-
" ry where encouraged, quickened and
" made effectual: And that all Convicti-
" ons affoon as they fhall be perfected,
" be forthwith certified into the *Exche-*
" *quer,* and that fpeedy procefs do iffue
" upon all fuch Convictions as are or fhall
" be certified : And that Care be taken,
" that no Perfons of Quality, who fhall
" be fufpected to be *Popifh* Recufants, be
" omitted to be prefented : And that no
" delay be ufed, nor any practice fuffer-
" ed, which may hinder or obftruct the
" compleating of fuch Convictions as are
" now preparing. And we do ftrictly
" Charge and Command, that no Mafs
" be faid in any Part of this Kingdom, the
" Chapels of our deareft Confort the Queen,
" and the Chapels of Foreign Minifters
" only excepted. And to prevent all ex-
" traordinary refort to thofe Chapels, by
" fuch who are not Menial Servants to
" the Queen, or to Foreign Minifters, we
" declare, that every fuch Offender fhall
" incur

" incur the Forfeiture of One Hundred
" Marks, provided by the Statute made
" in the Twenty Third Year of Queen
" Elizabeth, whereof one Third Part
" shall be given to the Informer for his far-
" ther Reward and Encouragement. And
" we require all Officers and Ministers of
" Justice to cause diligent Search to be
" made in all other Places where they shall
" hear or suspect that Mass is said, and to
" cause all Offenders in this kind to be ap-
" prehended and proceeded with according
" to Law. And we forewarn all our Sub-
" jects, that they presume not to send any
" Person to be educated Abroad in any Po-
" pish College or Seminary; and we com-
" mand all Parents or Guardians of any
" Person or Persons, now remaining in
" any such College or Seminary, that they
" cause the said Person or Persons speedi-
" ly to return home, as they will answer
" the contrary at their Peril. Moreover,
" we require all Persons born in any of
" our Dominions, and out of Prison, who
" have taken Orders by any Authority de-
" rived from the Church or See of *Rome*
" (except Mr. *John Huddleston*) to depart
" the Kingdom before the Twenty Fifth
" Day of *March* next, according to the
" Tenor of our late Proclamation; and
" also to depart the Court within the
" Fourteen Days appointed by our late

D   " Or-

" Order in Council. And we forbid all
" Papifts, or reputed Papifts, to come in-
" to our Palaces at *Whitehall* or St. *James's,*
" or into any other Place where our Court
" fhall be, contrary to our late Prohibiti-
" on, upon pain of Imprifonment in the
" *Tower,* if he be a Peer of the Realm;
" or in fome other Prifon if he be of lef-
" fer Quality. And Laftly, we appoint,
" that care be taken for the Suppreffion of
" Conventicles, hereby declaring that all
" our Licences were long fince recalled,
" and that no Conventicle hath any Au-
" thority, Allowance, or Encouragement
" from us. And our Pleafure is, that
" thefe our Commands be publifhed and
" proclaimed in the ufual manner.

" *Given at our Court at* Whitehall *this*
" *Twelfth Day of* February, *in the*
" *Twenty feventh Year of our Reign.*

This Declaration referred to an Order in
Council made on the Third Day of *Febru-*
ary, wherein the King upon advifing with
feveral of his Bifhops, agreed upon Six
Orders and Refolutions then taken for the
more effectual Conviction of Popifh Recufants, and the Suppreffion of Conventicles:
Of which the laft was this, *And his Majefty*
doth farther Order and Appoint, that effe-
ctual Care be taken for the Suppreffion of Con-
venticles:

venticles : And whereas divers pretend Licences from his Majesty, and would support themselves by that pretence, his Majesty declares, That all his Licences were long since recalled ; and that no Conventicle hath any Authority, Allowance, or Encouragement from his Majesty. The Nonconformists on this Occasion thus partially expressed themselves. His Majesty called the Bishops up to *London*, to give him Advice what was to be done for the securing of Religion, *&c.* and they after divers Consultations with the Ministers of State, advised him to recall his Licences, and put the Laws against the Nonconformists in Execution ; and this was done by a Declaration and Proclamation, declaring the Licences long since void, and requiring the Execution of the Laws against Papists and Conventicles. No sooner was the Proclamation published, but special Informers were set on work to promote the Execution. A little before the Licences were recalled, Mr. *Baxter* openly declared in his Pulpit, *That it was not in Opposition to the publick Churches that he kept up a Meeting, but to help the People in their Necessity, who were many more than the Parish Church could hold.* Hereupon it was confidently reported that he was Conforming ———. Another Session of Parliament approaching, Bishop MORLEY and Bishop WARD were in appearance very sensible of Popery, and there-

Case of the Dissenters as represented by themselves

fore very forward for Abatements, and taking in the Nonconformists, and moved it to many. At length Dr. TILLOTSON and Dr. STILLINGFLEET defired a Meeting with Dr. MANTON, Dr. BATES, Mr. POOL, and Mr. BAXTER, in order to confider of an Accommodation, and faid they had the Encouragement of feveral Lords both Spiritual and Temporal. Mr. BAXTER at firft met the two Doctors alone; and they confidered and canvaffed various Draughts, and at length fixed on one in which they agreed. This being communicated to the Nonconformists, was agreeable; but when they communicated it to the Bifhops, there was an end of the Treaty. A great many Things could not be obtained, upon which Mr. BAXTER fent to Dr. TILLOTSON, to know whether he might have leave to fpeak of it, in order to the promoting Concord, and to fignifie how far they were agreed, that their Names might be fome Advantage to the Work, and he thereupon returned him the following Letter, dated *April* 11. 1675.

SIR,

I Took *the firft Opportunity after you were with us, to fpeak to the Bifhop of* Salisbury, *who promifed to keep the Matter private, and only to acquaint the Bifhop of* Chichefter *with it in order to a Meeting; but upon fome general Dif-*

Discourse I plainly perceived several Things could not be obtained. However, he promis'd to appoint a Time of Meeting, but I have not heard from him since. I am unwilling my Name should be used in this Matter, not but that I do most heartily desire an Accommodation, and shall always endeavour it; but I am sure it will be a Prejudice to me, and signifie nothing to the effecting of the Thing, which as Circumstances are, cannot pass in either House without the Concurrence of a considerable part of the Bishops, and the Countenance of his Majesty, which at present I see little Reason to expect.

I am
        Your affectionate Brother
            and Servant,
                J. TILLOTSON.

The Terms agreed on were much of the same Nature with those delivered the Year before by Mr. BAXTER to the Earl of OR-RERY; the Chief of which were these,

" That no Covenant, Promise, or Oath, *Proposals*
" should be required to Ordination, Insti-*for a Uni-*
" tution, or Induction, but the Oaths of *on between Confor-*
" Allegiance and Supremacy. The Sub-*mists and*
" scribing to the Doctrine and Sacraments *Noncon-formists.*
" of the Church of *England*, as express'd
" in the 39 Articles, and a general Decla-
" ration against Rebellion and Sedition.
" That till the Nonconformists could be

        D 3   " bet-

" better provided for by Vacancies, they
" fhould have Liberty to be School-
" Mafters, or Affiftants to Incumbents,
" or to preach Lectures in their Churches;
" either fuch Lectures as were already en-
" dow'd with Maintenance, or fuch as the
" People fhould be willing to maintain;
" and that in the mean time their Meeting
" Places that were convenient, fhould be
" continued in ufe as Chapels. That Li-
" berty be allowed for Neighbours joyn-
" ing together in praying to God, and
" praifing him, and repeating Sermons,
" in their private Houfes without mole-
" ftation. That for the Liturgy, *&c.*
" none be obliged to read the Apocryphal
" Leffons: That it be enough if an Incum-
" bent once in a Quarter or Half Year,
" read the greateft part of the Service for
" that Time; and that it be at other times
" done by his Curate or Affiftant. That
" Lecturers be not obliged to read the Ser-
" vice; or at moft, that it be enough, if
" once in half a Year they read the great-
" eft part of what is appointed for that
" Time. That Parents have Liberty to
" dedicate their own Children to God in
" Baptifm, without being obliged to find
" Godfathers and Godmothers. That the
" Ufe of the Sign of the Crofs be left to
" the Minifters Inclination and Difcretion.
" That Minifters be not forced to baptize
                                   " a

" a Child whose Parents are denied the
" Communion of the Church, unless some
" serious Christian undertake for its Edu-
" cation, according to the Christian Cove-
" nant. That none be forced to receive
" the Sacrament while unfit or averse.
" That Ministers be not forced to deliver
" the Sacrament to any unbaptized Per-
" sons : Or to such as will not own their
" baptismal Covenant, and publickly pro-
" fess their Adherence to it; or to such as
" are guilty of scandalous Immoralities,
" till they have professed Repentance.
" That Ministers be not forced to publish
" an Excommunication, or Absolution a-
" gainst their Consciences, upon the De-
" cree of a Lay-Chancellor, &c. or har-
" rass'd by attending their Courts, to
" bring Witnesses against those to whom
" they have refused the Sacrament upon
" the aforesaid Reasons. That it be left
" to the Discretion of Ministers, whom
" they will absolve in Sickness, and to
" whom they will give the Sacrament,
" and over whom they at their Interment
" will use those few Words which import
" the Justification and Salvation of the
" deceased : And that the Sick and Dying
" have the liberty of choosing what Mini-
" sters they will to attend and assist them
" without restraint. That no Ministers
" be forced to deny the Sacrament to such

D 4 " as

" as think it unlawful to take it kneeling.
" That the Use of the Surplice be left in-
" different. And that People who live
" under an ignorant or scandalous Mini-
" ster, have liberty to joyn with those
" with whom they can better profit, in
" any neighbouring Church in the same
" Diocese, paying the Incumbent his dues.
" That no ordained Ministers be put up-
" on renouncing their Ordination, but
" upon Proof of their fitness for the Mi-
" nistry, receive by Word, or a written
" Instrument, a legal Authority to exer-
" cise their Ministry in any Congregation
" in his Majesty's Dominions, where they
" shall be lawfully called. That no ex-
" communicate Person as such, be impri-
" soned or ruined. And that after all,
" Christian Lenity be used to all consci-
" entious Dissenters; and that the tolera-
" ble be tolerated, under Laws of Peace
" and Safety. Upon the whole he added,
" That if the Sacraments were but left
" free to be administred, and received by
" none but Voluntiers ; and Liberty grant-
" ed to Ministers to preach in those
" Churches where the Common Prayer
" was read by others: And the Subscrip-
" tions contained nothing that a conscien-
" tious Man might need to scruple: He
" thought it might take in all, even the
" *Independents* as well as *Presbyterians.*"

                                        Mr.

Mr. BAXTER gave the Earl of *Orrery* theſe Propoſals; but he, after ſome time, re-turn'd them with Biſhop MORLEY's Stri-ctures and Animadverſions upon them, and they came to nothing.

I have already acquainted the Reader, *He publiſh-es Biſhop* that Biſhop WILKINS at his Death, was *Wilkins* pleaſed by his laſt Will to commit all his *his Book* Papers to Dr. TILLOTSON's Care and Dif- *of Natural Religion.* poſal, out of which, in the Year 1675. he publiſhed that learned Treatiſe, *Of the Principles and Duties of Natural Religion,* in Two Books, with an excellent Preface, giving an Account of the Work. Every thing this eloquent and learned Prelate has writ, is of ſuch ineſtimable Value, that it would be an irreparable Loſs to the Pub-lick, ſhould one Word of his Works be forgotten : Therefore I hope it will not be thought improper to inſert at large that uſeful prefatory Diſcourſe which he pre-fixed to this excellent Book ; alſo his Pre-faces to the pious and learned Dr. BAR-ROW's Works, and Mr. HEZEKIAH BUR-TON's Diſcourſes, which he likewiſe pub-liſhed.

The Preface to the *Principles of Natural Religion* is as follows :

' THE enſuing *Treatiſe* is ſufficiently *Preface to* ' recommended to the World by *Bp Wil-kins's* ' the Name of the *Author,* and needs no- *Natural Religion.* ' thing

' thing elfe to make Way for its Enter-
' tainment. I fhall only therefore give a
' fhort Account of thefe *Remains* of that
' Learned and Excellent *Perfon*, and of
' the particular Defign and Intention of
' them.

' He was pleafed by his *laft Will* to com-
' mit his *Papers* to my Care, and out of his
' great Friendfhip, and undeferved good
' Opinion of me, to leave it wholly to my
' Difpofal, whether any, or what Part of
' them fhould be made publick. *This*
' *Treatife*, I knew, he always defign'd for
' that Purpofe ; and if God had been plea-
' fed to have granted him but a little lon-
' ger Life, he would have publifhed it
' himfelf: And therefore, tho' a confide-
' rable Part of it wanted his laft Hand, yet
' neither could I be fo injurious, to de-
' prive the World of it, becaufe it was lefs
' perfect than he intended it ; nor durft I
' be fo bold, to attempt to *finifh* a *Piece* de-
' figned and carried on fo far by fo great
' a *Mafter.*

' The firft *Twelve Chapters* were writ-
' ten out for the Prefs in his Life-time.
' The *Remainder* hath been gather'd and
' made up out of his *Papers*, as well as the
' *Materials* left for that Purpofe, and the
' Skill of the *Compiler* would allow: So
' that it cannot be expected, that the *Work*
' fhould be of equal Strength and Beauty
'in

' in all the Parts of it. However, such
' as it is, I hope it may prove of considera-
' ble Use and Benefit to the World, and
' not altogether unworthy of its *Author*.

' The *Design* of it is threefold.

' *First*, To establish the great *Principles*
' of *Religion*, the *Being of God*, and a *Fu-*
' *ture State* ; by shewing how firm and so-
' lid a Foundation they have in the Na-
' ture and Reason of Mankind ; a Work
' never more necessary than in this dege-
' nerate Age, which hath been so misera-
' bly over-run with *Scepticism* and *Infide-*
' *lity*.

' *Secondly*, To convince Men of the *na-*
' *tural* and indispensable Obligation of *Mo-*
' *ral Duties* ; those I mean which are com-
' prehended by our *Saviour*, under the
' two general *Heads* of *the Love of God*,
' and *of our Neighbour*. For all the great
' *Duties* of *Piety and Justice* are written up-
' on our Hearts, and every Man feels a se-
' cret Obligation to them in his own Con-
' science, which checks and restrains him
' from doing contrary to them, and gives
' him Peace and Satisfaction in the Dis-
' charge of his Duty ; or in case he offend
' against it, fills him with Guilt and Ter-
' ror.

' And certainly it is a thing of very con-
' siderable Use, rightly to understand the
' natural Obligation of Moral Duties, and
                                    ' how

' how neceffarily they flow from the Con-
' fideration of *God*, and of *our felves*. For
' it is a great Miftake, to think that the
' Obligation of them doth folely depend
' upon the Revelation of God's Will made
' to us in the *Holy Scriptures*. It is plain
' that Mankind was always under a *Law*,
' even before God had made any external
' and extraordinary Revelation; elfe, how
' fhall God judge the World? how fhall
' they to whom the *Word of God* never
' came, be acquitted or condemn'd at the
' *Great Day?* For *where there is no Law*,
' there can neither be *Obedience* nor *Tranf-*
' *greffion.*

 ' It is indeed an unfpeakable Advantage
' which we who are *Chriftians* do enjoy,
' both in refpect of the more clear and cer-
' tain Knowledge of our Duty in all the
' Branches of it; and likewife in regard of
' the powerful Motives and Affiftance
' which our bleffed *Saviour* in his *Gofpel*
' offers to us, to enable and encourage us
' to the Difcharge of our Duty. But yet
' it is neverthelefs very ufeful for us to
' confider the primary and natural Obliga-
' tion to *Piety* and *Virtue*, which we com-
' monly call the *Law of Nature*; this being
' every whit as much the *Law of God*, as
' the *Revelation* of his Will in his *Word*;
' and confequently, nothing contained in
' the *Word of God*, or in any pretended *Re-*
       ' *velation*

' *velation* from *Him*, can be interpreted
' to diffolve the Obligation of moral Du-
' ties plainly required by the Law of Na-
' ture. And if this one Thing were but
' well confider'd, it would be an effectual
' Antidote againft the pernicious Doctrines
' of the *Antinomians*, and of all other *Li-*
' *bertine-Enthufiafts* whatfoever : Nothing
' being more incredible, than that *Divine*
' *Revelation* fhould contradict the clear
' and unqueftionable Dictates of *Natural*
' *Light* ; nor any Thing more vain, than
' to fancy that the *Grace of God* does releafe
' Men from the *Laws of Nature*.

  ' This the *Author* of the following *Dif-*
' *courfes* was very fenfible of; and wifely
' faw of what Confequence it was to efta-
' blifh the *Principles* and *Duties* of Religion
' upon their true and natural Foundation ;
' which is fo far from being a Prejudice to
' *Divine Revelation*, that it prepares the
' way for it, and gives it greater Advan-
' tage and Authority over the Minds of
' Men.

  ' *Thirdly*, To perfwade Men to the *Pra-*
' *ctice* of *Religion*, and the *Vertues* of a good
' Life, by fhewing how natural and direct
' an Influence they have, not only upon
' our *future* Bleffednefs in another World,
' but even upon the Happinefs and Profpe-
' rity of this *prefent* Life. And furely no-
' thing is more likely to prevail with wife
                                    ' and

' and confiderate Men to become Religi-
' ous, than to be thoroughly convinced,
' that *Religion* and *Happiness*, our *Duty* and
' our *Interest*, are really but one and the
' fame Thing confidered under feveral No-
' tions.

J. TILLOTSON.

Would not Sign an Address, &c.

In the Year 1680 the Houfe of Commons finding no other way to keep Popery out of the Nation, than by excluding the Duke of YORK from the Succeffion to the Crown, they brought in a Bill to difable him. On *November* the 11th it paffed the Commons; on the 15th it was carried up to the Lords by the Lord RUSSEL, and there at the fecond Reading it was thrown out by a Majority of Thirty Voices, of which Fourteen were Bifhops. Upon this the Clergy in and about the City of *London* prefented an Addrefs of Thanks to the King for not agreeing to the Bill of Exclufion, which Dr. TILLOTSON refufed to fign.

Gives Fifty Pounds towards Printing the Bible and Common-Prayer Book in the Welch Tongue.

In the Year 1681 died the Reverend and Pious Mr. GOUGE, of whom Dr. TILLOTSON in his Funeral Sermon gives this excellent Character, *viz.* " That he was of " a Difpofition ready to embrace and o- " blige all Men; allowing others to differ " from him, even in Opinions that were " very dear to him; and provided Men
" did

" did but fear God, and work Righteouf-
" nefs, he loved them heartily, how di-
" ftant foever from him in Judgment a-
" bout Things lefs neceffary: In all which
" he is very worthy to be a Pattern for
" Men of all Perfwafions whatfoever.
Mr. GOUGE was a Perfon of an uncommon Piety and Charity, and an indefatiga-
ble Diligence in doing good. That which
gives Occafion to mention him here, is,
that he procured the *Church Catechifm*,
The Practice of Piety; and that beft of Books,
The whole Duty of Man; befides feveral o-
ther pious and ufeful Treatifes, to be tranflated into the *Welch* Tongue, and great
Numbers of them to be printed, and fent
down to the chief Towns in *Wales*, to be
fold at eafie Rates to thofe that were able
to buy them, and to be freely given to
thofe that were not. But that which was
the greateft Work of all, and amounted indeed to a mighty Charge, he procured a
new and very fair Impreffion of the Bible
and Liturgy of the Church of *England* in
the *Welch* Tongue (the former Impreffion
being difpers'd, and hardly Twenty of them
to be had in all *London*) to the Number of
Eight Thoufand : One Thoufand whereof
were freely given to the Poor, and the reft
fent to the principal Cities and Towns in
Wales, to be fold to the Rich at very reafonable and low Rates, *viz.* at Four Shillings a
Piece

Piece well bound and clapfed; which was much cheaper than any *English* Bible was ever fold that was of fo fair a Print and Paper. Towards the carrying on this charitable Work, large and bountiful Contributions (chiefly by his Induftry and prudent Application) were obtained from charitable Perfons of all Ranks and Conditions, from the Nobility and Gentry of *Wales* and the neighbouring Countries, and feveral of that Quality in and about *London*: From divers of the Right Reverend Bifhops, and of the Clergy; amongft the reft, Dr. TILLOTSON (then Dean of St. *Paul's*) was a great promoter of this good and charitable Undertaking, and contributed towards it Fifty Pounds. And indeed it was a Work of that Charge, that it was not likely to have been done any other way; and for which this Age, and perhaps the next, will have great caufe to thank God on his behalf.

Preface to Bp Wilkins's Sermons. In the Year 1682. he laid a farther Obligation upon the Publick, by giving them a Volume of excellent Sermons, confifting of Fifteen in Number, from Bifhop WILKINS's Papers, to which he prefix'd the following Preface:

' I Eafily forefee, that in this cenforious ' and inquifitive Age, *two* Queftions ' will be asked concerning the publifhing
' of

‘ of these Sermons, *Why no sooner ?* or *Why*
‘ *at all ?* since so many come abroad every
‘ Day, that the Age is almost opprest with
‘ them. To the *first* I answer, Because I
‘ was not at leisure before to review them,
‘ and to get them transcribed out of a Hand
‘ not legible enough for the Press. To the
‘ *other*, Because though there be many Ser-
‘ mons, yet not many such; whether we
‘ consider in them the Usefulness and
‘ Weight of the Matters treated of ; or the
‘ suitable Manner of handling them, in a
‘ Stile of so much Clearness, and Close-
‘ ness, and Strength, as was fitted (as he
‘ himself was wont to wish) *to the Capacity*
‘ *of the weakest, and the Conviction of the*
‘ *strongest* ; or the solid and well-poiz’d Judg-
‘ ment of the Author in Points of Diffi-
‘ culty ; or lastly, the admirable Candour
‘ and Moderation of his Temper in Mat-
‘ ters of Difference and Dispute.

 ‘ And I purposely mention his *Modera-* *Bishop*
‘ *tion*, and likewise adventure to commend *Wilkin's*
‘ him for it ; notwithstanding that this *Character.*
‘ *Virtue*, so much esteemed and magnified
‘ by wise Men in all Ages, hath of late been
‘ declaimed against with so much Zeal
‘ and Fierceness, and yet with that good
‘ Grace and Confidence, as if it were not
‘ only no *Virtue*, but even the Sum and
‘ Abridgment of all *Vices*. I say, notwith-
‘ standing all this, I am still of the old
     E   ‘ Opinion,

' Opinion, That *Moderation* is a *Virtue,*
' and one of the peculiar Ornaments and
' Advantages of the excellent Conftitution
' of our Church, and muft at laft be the
' Temper of her Members, efpecially the
' Clergy, if ever we ferioufly intend the
' firm Eftablifhment of this Church, and
' do not induftrioufly defign by cherifhing
' Heats and Divifions among our felves,
' to let in Popery at thefe Breaches.

' As to the *Author* himfelf, I cannot
' forbear out of a generous Indignation to
' fee the Afhes of fo worthy a Man tram-
' pled upon, to take Notice of a very flight,
' and, I think, unjuft Character given of
' him in a late Book, entituled, *Hiftoria*
' *& Antiquitates Univerfitatis Oxonienfis;*
' whether by the Author of that Book, or
' by fome other Hand, is varioufly report-
' ed, and I am not curious to know.
' The former Part of the Character is
' chiefly made up of invidious Reflections
' upon his Carriage, and the Circumftan-
' ces of his Condition in the late Times;
' in all which, becaufe I did not then
' know him, I leave him to be vindicated
' or cenfured by thofe who were Witnef-
' fes of his whole Behaviour and Temper
' in that Time. The latter Part of it con-
' fifts of flat and ill-favour'd Commenda-
' tions; as, That he was *Philofophiæ &*
' *Mathematica addictiffimus,* a great Well-
'   ' willer

' Willet to Philoſophy and the Mathema-
' ticks; the exact Character of an *Empi-*
' *rick* and an *Almanack-maker*, when theſe
' two Excellencies happen to be in Con-
' junction! And then, that *to the Study of Di-*
' *vinity he added, Eloquentiam in concienan-*
' *do non contemnendam, an Eloquence in*
' *Preaching not to be deſpiſed*; which though
' it be but a very cold and ſlender Com-
' mendation both of his Divinity and his
' Eloquence, yet I muſt own ſomething
' of Kindneſs in it; becauſe there is in
' good earneſt a ſort of Eloquence in
' Preaching that is to be deſpiſed. To fi-
' niſh the Kindneſs, and that nothing
' might be omitted that might any ways
' caſt an *Odium* upon him, as he is placed
' next before Mr. Hobbes, ſo I cannot but
' obſerve in comparing their Characters,
' that there is apparently far leſs of Envy
' and Detraction in that of Mr. Hobbes,
' than in this of the reverend Biſhop; for
' which I can imagine no other Reaſon but
' this, that Mr. Hobbes was then alive to
' ſpeak for himſelf, but *the Dead bite not.*
    ' Upon the whole, it hath often been
' no ſmall Matter of Wonder to me,
' whence it ſhould come to paſs, that ſo
' great a Man, and ſo great a Lover of
' Mankind, who had the Inclination, the
' Skill, and the Opportunity to oblige ſo
' very many, and was ſo highly valued
        B 2   ' and

' and reverenced by all that knew him;
' should yet have the hard Fate to fall
' under the heavy Displeasure and Cen-
' sure of those who knew him not: And
' that he who never did any thing to make
' himself one personal Enemy, should have
' the ill Fortune to have so many. I think I
' may truly say, that there are, or have
' been, very few in this Age and Nation,
' so well known, and so greatly esteemed
' and favoured, first by a judicious Prince,
' and then by so many Persons of high
' Rank and Quality, and of singular
' Worth and Eminency in all the learned
' Professions, as our *Author* was.

' And this surely cannot be denied him,
' it is so well known to many worthy
' Persons yet living, and hath been so often
' acknowledged even by his Enemies, that
' in the late Times of Confusion, almost all
' that was preserved and kept up of Inge-
' nuity and Learning, of good Order and
' Government in the *University* of *Oxford*,
' was chiefly owing to his prudent Con-
' duct and Encouragement. Which Con-
' sideration alone, had there been no other,
' might have prevail'd with some there to
' have treated his Memory with at least
' common Kindness and Respect. Not to
' do this to the dead, and in Character of
' him that was intended to live to Poste-
' rity, seems very hard; and yet I shall
' only

' only make this foft Reflection upon it,
' That there is no readier Way for any
' Man to bring his own Worth into Que-
' ftion, than by endeavouring to detract
' from the univerfally acknowledged Worth
' of other Men.

' Having faid this out of Juftice as well
' as Friendfhip to the *Author*, and by way
' of neceffary Vindication of him, from the
' Envy endeavoured to be raifed againft
' him by fome in this prefent Age, I leave
' thefe *Difcourfes* of his to juftify them-
' felves and him to Pofterity.

J. TILLOTSON.

In 1683, My Lord RUSSEL was behead- *His Let-*
ed for Treafon, as was pretended ; but in *ter to my*
reality, for his vigorous Oppofition to Po- *Lord Ruf-*
pery and Arbitrary Government. During *in New-*
his Imprifonment, he was frequently vifi- *gate.*
ted by thofe Two learned Divines, Dr.
BURNETT, late Bifhop of *Sarum*, and our
moft excellent Primate. When that Lord
was under Condemnation, he writ him
the following Letter, which will fairly
clear him from a falfe Reprefentation made
of him as no Friend to that Doctrine of the
Church of *England*, *Paffive Obedience*.

E 3   My

My Lord,

I Was heartily glad to see your Lordship this
Morning in that calm and devout Temper
at the receiving the Blessed Sacrament; but
Peace of Mind unless it be well grounded, will
avail little: And because transient Discourse
many Times hath little Effect for want of Time
to weigh and confider it, therefore in tender
Compassion of your Lordship's Case, and from
all the Good-Will that one Man can bear to another, I do humbly offer to your Lordship's deli-
berate Thoughts these following Considerations
concerning the Points of Resistance; If our
Religion and Rights should be invaded, as
your Lordship puts the Case, concerning which
I understand by Dr. BURNETT that your Lordship had once received Satisfaction, and am sorry
to find a Change.

First, That the Christian Religion doth
plainly forbid the Resistance of Authority.

Secondly, That tho' our Religion be Establish'd by Law (which your Lordship urges as
a Difference between our Case and that of the
Primitive Christians) yet in the same Law
which Establishes our Religion it is declar'd,
That it is not Lawful upon any Pretence
whatsoever to take up Arms, &c. Besides
that, there is a particular Law declaring the
Power of the Militia to be solely in the King.
And that ties the Hands of Subjects, tho' the

Law

Law of Nature, and the General Rules of Scripture had left us at Liberty; which I believe they do not; because the Government and Peace of Human Society could not well subsist upon those Terms.

Thirdly, *Your Lordship's Opinion is contrary to the* declared Doctrine of all Proteſtant Churches; *and tho' some particular Persons have taught otherwise, yet they have been* contradicted *herein, and* condemned *for it by the generality of Protestants: And I beg your Lordship to consider, how it will agree with an avowed Asserting of the* Proteſtant Religion, *to go contrary to the* General Doctrine of Proteſtants. *My End in this is to convince your Lordship, that you are in a very great and dangerous Mistake; and being so convinced, that which before was a Sin of Ignorance, will appear of a much more heinous Nature, as in Truth it is, and call for a very particular and deep Repentance; which if your Lordship sincerely exercise upon the sight of your* Error, *by a penitent Acknowledgment of it to God and Men, You will not only obtain Forgiveness of God, but prevent a mighty* Scandal *to the* Reformed Religion. *I am very loth to give your Lordship any Disquiet in the Distress you are in, which I commiserate from my Heart, but am much more concerned that you do not leave the* World *in a* Delusion *and false Peace, to the hindrance of your Eternal Happiness. I heartily pray for* You, *and beseech your Lordship*

to

*to believe that I am with the greatest Sincerity,
and Compassion in the World,*

My Lord,
Your Lordſhip's moſt faithful
July 20,   and afflicted Servant,
1683.   J. TILLOTSON.

And in his laſt Prayer with his Lordſhip
on the Scaffold, he thus concludes, *Grant
Lord, that all we who ſurvive, by this and other
Inſtances of thy Providence, may learn our Duty
to God and the King.* What could a Man
have ſaid more in behalf of any Doctrine
of the Church of *England?* And tho' he
did comply with the Revolution, yet it is
moſt certain that he never changed his O-
pinion in this Point, altho' his Enemies
charge him with * *Apoſtacy from his once a-
vowed Principle and Doctrine of the Church
of* England, *the once venerable Doctrine of
Non-Reſiſtance and Paſſive-Obedience: In
which our Church hath taught her Children
how they ſhould behave themſelves towards
Men, and approve themſelves towards God,
if ſhe and they ſhould come to be perſecuted for
the Trial of their Faith, as the pureſt Churches
and beſt Chriſtians have been in former Ages.*

I

---

* *See a Pamphlet entituled,* Some Diſcourſes upon Dr.
Burnett and Dr. *Tillotſon,* &c. p. 35.

I cannot make a better Reply to this Accusation, than in the Words of the late learned Bishop of *Sarum*, in his Answer to the foresaid Pamphlet, which does undeniably prove that here was no Change of Principles, nor departing from former Opinions.

" As I have (*says his Lordship*) ex-
" presly and publickly owned a re-
" serve for Resistance in case of a *To-*
" *tal Subversion*; so I must add, that to
" my knowledge, other Divines still un-
" derstood that Doctrine of *Non-Resistance*
" with this Reserve; though they did
" not think it necessary to mention it. If
" a Man were to exhort married Persons
" to their Duty, he might use that gene-
" ral Expression of St. *Paul, That the Hus-*
" *band is the Head of the Wife, even as*
" *Christ is the Head of the Church*; and that
" as *the Church is subject unto Christ, so*
" *Wives ought to be subject to their own Hus-*
" *bands in every Thing*: He might say all
" this, without an Exception; and yet in
" the Case of intolerable Cruelty, the
" Wife may see to her own Preservation;
" but *Desertion* or *Adultery* sets her more
" at liberty. In the same manner, when
" we exhort Children to *obey their Parents*
" *in all things*; we do not suppose the Case
" of their Parents going about to kill them,
" nor argue what they may do in such a
                                        " Case.

" Cafe. Extraordinary Cafes ought not
" to be fuppofed, when we give the Dire-
" &ions that belong to the ordinary Courfe
" of Life ; and therefore Divines might
" preach Submiffion in very large and full
" Expreffions, who yet might believe,
" That *a Total Subverfion* was a Cafe of a-
" nother Nature, which might warrant
" more violent Remedies. This I am fure
" was our late Primate's Opinion. This
" was that which we laid before that
" Great, but innocent Victim, that was
" facrificed to the Rage of a Party, I
" mean the Lord *Ruffell*, who was con-
" demned for *Treafonable Words*, tho' there
" was not one Witnefs that fwore one
" *Word* againft him ; it being only depo-
" fed, That *Treafonable Words* were faid
" in his Hearing; to which, as was fworn,
" he was confenting, tho' no *Words* of His
" were expreffed, that imported any fuch
" Confent. The true Cafe of that whole
" Matter was ftated thus ; A vifible De-
" fign was carried on to bring in *Popery*
" and *Arbitrary Government*. In order to
" that, *Quo Warranto's* were brought a-
" gainft feveral Cities and Burroughs,
" which would have changed the Confti-
" tution of the Houfe of Commons ; and
" *Sheriffs* unduly elected were put on the
" City of *London*, on Defign, as 'twas be-
" lieved, to pack Juries. Thefe things
                                      " were

" were thought juft Grounds of Refiftance ;
" the late Primate and my felf were of a-
" nother Opinion; We knew, or at leaft
" had Reafon to believe we knew, the Se-
" cret of the King's Religion who then
" reigned ; and did not doubt of the bad
" Defigns that were then on Foot, and of
" the illegal Actings of that Time ; yet
" we ftill thought that remote Fears and
" Confequences, together with illegal Pra-
" ctifes, did not juftify *Refiftance* ; but
" that the Laws both of the Gofpel and of
" the Land, did bind us in that Cafe to
" Submiffion. That Lord upon this, faid,
" *He did not fee a Difference between a Legal*
" *and a Turkiſh Conſtitution, upon this Hy-*
" *potheſis:* And when we told him, That
" *a Total Subverſion* changed the Cafe ; he
" anfwered, *Then it would be too late to re-*
" *ſiſt.* In all that Affair the late Primate
" had the fame Opinion, and no other than
" that he had to the laft. Some particu-
" lar Confiderations reftrained him from
" Writing about it ; but he did not de-
" cline to explain this, as oft as there was
" Occafion given for it.

" Upon the whole Matter, there are
" two Queftions in the Point of *Refiftance* :
" The one is, Whether Subjects may Re-
" ſiſt meerly upon the Account of *Religi-*
" *on,* or not, either to force a General
" Reformation, or to fecure themfelves
                                        " from

" from Perfecution? The other is con-
" cerning the Conftitution of States and
" Kingdoms; and of this in particular,
" How far they have retained or loft their
" Liberties? The one is a Point of Divi-
" nity, the other is a Point of Law and
" Hiftory. As to the firft, I do not know
" one of all the Divines that have fworn
" to the prefent Government, who are not
" ftill of the fame Opinion that they were
" formerly of, and that do not ftill judge
" *Refiftance* on the Account of Religion to
" be unlawful. Nor does it any way re-
" flect on them, if they fhould have chan-
" ged their Opinion in the other Point,
" which falls not fo properly within their
" Studies. They might have been mifled
" by Chimerical Notions of *Imperial and*
" *Political Laws*; they might have thought
" that the Zeal with which fome had pro-
" mifed to ftand it out againft a Popifh
" King, threatning that they would tell
" him to his Face (at leaft owning that
" it was their Duty to do it) That he was
Jovian, " an *Idolater,* a *Bread-Worfhipper,* a *God-*
p. 96. " *defs-Worfhipper*; with a great many other
" fine Names, that they faid they would
" give him. They might, I fay, have
" thought, that we were fafe under the
" Conduct of Men, who were fo bold
" when there was no Danger; but were
" much tamer and more cautious as the
                                        " Dan-

" Danger came nearer them. Thus many
" might go into wrong Notions of our
" Government, and think we had no Li-
" berties left us, but what were at the
" Difcretion of our Princes. It is no De-
" rogation from the Learning and Studies
" of Divines to own, that tho' they are
" ftill of their former Opinion in that
" which is Theological, and that was on-
" ly incumbent on them to know ; yet in
" Matters of Law and Policy, they might
" have been led into Miftakes. This an-
" fwers all that pompous Objection, with
" which fo much Noife is made, and up-
" on which fo many ill Words have been
" faftened. A great many have not at all
" changed their Opinion, even in this fe-
" cond Point ; and others do fee that they
" were miftaken in their Opinion concern-
" ing our Conftitution, and the Nature
" of Laws and Legal Security ; and the
" Right that arifes out of thefe, in the
" Cafe of a *Total Subverfion.*

He has been alfo reprefented as no lover
of the Liturgy of the Church of *England.*
Dr. CALAMY tells the following Story of *Calamy's*
him. ' Dr. TILLOTSON frankly owning in *Abridg-ment of*
' a Sermon, that the Diffenters had fome *Mr.* Bax-
' plaufible Objections againft the Com- *ter's Hi-*
' mon-Prayer, Arch-Bifhop *Sancroft* fend- *ftory, &c.*
' ing for him to reprimand him, he ftood *p. 226.*
' to what he had afferted: The Arch-Bi-
' fhop

' shop asked him which parts of the Com-
' mon-Prayer he meant; and he men-
' tioned the *Burial Office*; upon which
' that Arch-Bishop owned to him that he
' was so little satisfied with that *Office*
' himself, that for that very Reason he had
' never taken a Cure of Souls.' And because the Truth of this Story has been
called in Question, Dr. CALAMY says that
he had it under the Hand of Mr. STAN-
CLIFE, who wrote that Passage in the
Margin of his Abridgment, and afterwards was so kind as to send him the
Book for his own use. I shall not contest
the Truth of this Story, let it be true or
false; this worthy Prelate's Zeal and Affection for the Church of *England* will suf-
ficiently appear by the great Numbers
he brought over to her Communion.
The Author of the forementioned Pamphlet cannot bear it, that he should be
thought to have turned so great a part of
the City to love the Church: He thinks he
did it not: That he only perswaded Men
to bear with the Church, but not to love
it, or become zealous for it, as the Con-
verts of others have shewed themselves to
be. As for this, I appeal to all who knew
what the City was in 1662, and what it
was brought to in 1682, when those viru-
lent Men began to let loose their Malice a-
gainst this Great Man. There are too
many

many Witneffes to this, therefore he cannot quite deny it ; *but thefe Men,* fays he,
did not become Zealots ; that is, they did
not rail at, nor inform againft their old
Friends ; this is in our Author's Senfe to be
hearty for the Church : But as for thofe
who do ftill fincerely adhere to the Communion of our Church, and love it, all
who know the City will be forward to
own, that whoever gained their Thoufands, our late Primate gained his Ten
Thoufands.

    This Year he publifhed the Works of the *He pub-*
learned Dr. ISAAC BARROW, Mafter of *lifbeth Dr.*
Trinity College in *Cambridge.* And the *Barrow's and Mr.*
Year following he publifhed the Works of *Burton's*
his intimate Friend, the excellent Mr. HE- *Works.*
ZEKIAH BURTON, to both which Works
he writ the following Prefaces ; which
for Reafons before given I have here
inferted.

    'THE Author of the following Ser- *Preface*
      ' mons was fo publickly known, *to Dr.*
' and fo highly efteemed by all learned *Barrow's Works.*
' and good Men, that nothing either
' needs or can be faid more to his Ad-
' vantage. Not but that I think it very
' fit, that the Picture of this truly great
' Man fhould be drawn at full length, for
' the knowledge and imitation of Pofteri-
' ty ; and it will, I hope, be done here-
                    ' after

‘ of others, do not so properly belong to
‘ this Subject; but considering that this
‘ Vice is chiefly managed by the Tongue,
‘ and is almoſt ever attended with ſome
‘ irregularity and indiſcretion of Speech,
‘ they are not altogether ſo foreign and
‘ unſuitable to it. And never were Diſ-
‘ courſes of this kind more neceſſary than
‘ in this wicked and perverſe Generation;
‘ wherein the Vices here reprehended are
‘ ſo very rife, and out of the abundant
‘ Impiety of Men’s Hearts there proceeds
‘ ſo much *Evil-ſpeaking* of all Kinds, in
‘ atheiſtical Diſcourſes, and blaſpemous
‘ Raillery, and prophane Swearing; and
‘ when Cenſoriouſneſs, Detraction and
‘ Slander are ſcarce accounted Faults, even
‘ with thoſe who would ſeem to be moſt
‘ ſtrict in other Parts and Duties of Reli-
‘ gion.

‘ The *Author* of them, as he was ex-
‘ emplary in all manner of Converſation,
‘ ſo eſpecially in this part of it; being of
‘ all Men I ever had the happineſs to know,
‘ the cleareſt of this common guilt, and
‘ moſt free from *offending in Word*; com-
‘ ing as near as is poſſible for Human Frail-
‘ ty to do, to the perfect Idea of St. *James*
‘ his *perfect Man.* So that in theſe Excel-
‘ lent Diſcourſes of his he hath only tran-
‘ ſcribed his own Practice. All the Rules
‘ which he hath given he moſt religiouſly
‘ ob-

'observ'd himself, and was very uneasie
'when at any time he saw them transgres-
'sed by others in his Company.

'There is one Thing in them needs ex-
'cuse, namely, That several Things
'which are more briefly and summarily
'said in the First of those Sermons, about
'*Evil-speaking*, are repeated in some of the
'following Discourses: Which, because
'it could not well be avoided, but either
'by wholly leaving out the First Sermon,
'or very much mangling some of the rest,
'will, it is hoped, for that reason be easi-
'ly pardoned.

'The *Eight* following *Sermons* are like-
'wise sorted together, because they ex-
'plain and enforce the *Two* great Com-
'mandments of the Law, the *Love of*
'*God*, and *of our Neighbour.*

'The *Two* next were published by him-
'self, and only those *Two*. The *First* of
'them, about the *Duty and Reward of*
'*Bounty to the Poor*, was preach'd at the
'*Spital*, and publish'd at the desire of the
'*Lord Mayor* and *Court of Aldermen*
'This was received with universal Appro-
'bation; and perhaps there is nothing ex-
'tant in *Divinity* more perfect in its kind:
'It seems to have exhausted the whole
'Argument, and to have left no Conside-
'ration belonging to it untouch'd. The
'other, on the *Passion of our Blessed Savi-*

' *our,* was the laft he preach'd, but one;
' and, I think, the occafion of his Death,
' by a Cold he then got, which, in all
' probability, was the caufe of the Fever
' of which he died, to our unfpeakable
' lofs. This he fent to the Prefs himfelf,
' but did not live to fee it publifh'd.
' A The next part of this *Volume* is a brief
' Explication of the *Lord's Prayer,* the *De-*
' *calogue,* and the Doctrine of the *Sacra-*
' *ments.* It were to be wifh'd, that the
' *Creed* alfo had been explain'd by him
' in the fame manner; but that he hath
' handled in a larger way, in a great many
' excellent *Sermons* upon the feveral *Arti-*
' *cles* of it, wherein he hath not only ex-
' plain'd and confirm'd the great Doctrines
' of our Religion, but likewife fhewn
' what influence every Article of our
' Faith ought to have upon our Practice.
' Which *Difcourfes* make the *Second* Vo-
' lume of his Works.
' The laft part of this *Firft* Volume is his
' learned *Treatife* of the *Pope's Supremacy,*
' to which, becaufe there is prefix'd a *Pre-*
' *face,* giving a fhort Account of it, I need
' not here to fay any Thing farther of it.
' Befides thefe, the *Author* hath left ma-
' ny other excellent *Sermons,* upon feveral
' important and ufeful Subjects in *Divini-*
' *ty:* Befides a great many learned *Lectures*
' and *Treatifes* in the *Mathematicks;* and
' divers

' divers, excellent *Orations* and *Poems*, all
' in *Latin*. All which may, God willing,
' in convenient time be communicated to
' the Publick, to the great Advantage and
' Furtherance of Religion and Learning.

' In the mean time, I heartily recom-
' mend thefe *Sermons* which are already
' publifh'd to thy ferious perufal; and fhall
' only fay this of them, That as they want
' no other kind of Excellency, fo particu-
' larly they are animated throughout with
' fo genuine a Spirit of true Piety and
' Goodnefs, that he muft either be a per-
' fectly good, or prodigioufly bad Man,
' that can read them over without being
' the better for them.

J. TILLOTSON.

The Preface to Mr. BURTON's Practical
Difcourfes.

' I SHALL fpeak a little concerning the
' Author of the enfuing Difcourfes,
' and then leave them to fpeak for them-
' felves. For if they be good, they need
' no Commendatory Preface, and if they
' be not, they deferve none.

' I muft not fay much of him, be-
' caufe of the long and intimate Friend-
' fhip I had with him, which may render
' me fufpected of Partiality towards him:
' And indeed I need not, fince he was a

F 3

' Per-

' Perfon fo well known, both in the Uni-
' verfity of *Cambridge*, where he was bred,
' and was a Fellow of *Magdalen-College*
' there, and an eminent Tutor for many
' Years; And likewife here in *London*,
' where he fpent feveral Years of the laft
' part of his Life, and was intimately ac-
' quainted with the moft eminent Perfons of
' his own Profeffion. He was firft Chap-
' lain to the Right Honourable Sir *Orlando*
' *Bridgman*, Lord Keeper of the Great
' Seal; and afterwards Minifter of St.
' *George*'s in *Southwark*; where befides his
' conftant Pains in Preaching and Cate-
' chifing, He employ'd a great part of his
' Time in Offices and Acts of Charity;
' in Vifitation of the Sick, and a moft ten-
' der and compaffionate Care of the Poor,
' which in that Parifh were exceeding ma-
' ny, befides the Two great Prifons of the
' *King*'s *Bench* and *Marfhalfea*, which he
' often vifited; and beftowed there not
' only his own Charity, but all that by his
' Intereft and Solicitation he could obtain
' from others; by which means he not on-
' ly continually relieved, but every Year
' releafed a very confiderable Number of
' poor Prifoners for fmall Debts, to the great
' Comfort of many poor Families. This,
' together with his exemplary Converfati-
' on among them in all Humility and
' Kindnefs, and Meeknefs of Wifdom,
                                    ' made

' made him to be exceedingly beloved in
' his Parish during his continuance with
' them, and his departure from them to be
' as greatly lamented: For about a Year
' before his Death he was removed to
' *Barns*, not far from *London*; where he
' was seized upon by a very dangerous
' and malignant Fever, of which he died,
' and several of his Family.

' It pleafed the wife Providence of
' God, *Whofe Ways are not as our Ways, nor*
' *his Thoughts as our Thoughts,* to take this
' good Man from us in the ripenefs of his
' Age, when he was capable of doing the
' greatest Service to the Church of God,
' and in a Time when he was moft likely
' to have contributed confiderably to it,
' as being by the incomparable Sweetnefs
' of his Temper, and Prudence of his Be-
' haviour, admirably fitted to allay thofe
' Heats which then began to break out,
' but are fince blown up to all the Degrees
' of a violent and implacable Enmity, by
' the skill and induftry of a crafty and reft-
' lefs Party among us, playing upon our
' Weaknefs, and perfwading us to receive
' odious Names of Diftinction, and to
' fling them like Squibs and Fire-balls at
' one another, to make the *Philiftines*
' fport. So that we have great Reafon to
' lament the Lofs of fo ufeful a Man in fo
' needful a Time.

' I

' I shall only mention those good Quali-
' ties and Virtues which were more re-
' markable in him. His great Piety to-
' wards God, the Native Simplicity of
' his Mind and Manners, the singular
' Kindness of his Conversation, and his
' cheerful readiness to every good Work:
' But above all, the Sincerity of his Friend-
' ship, for I never knew any Man that up-
' on all Occasions served his Friend with
' that Forwardness and Zeal, and unweari-
' ed Diligence as he would do, and with
' less Consideration of himself and his own
' Interest. He was infinitely troubled to
' see the abounding of Iniquity, and the
' abatement of Charity among us; but
' he did not live to see the worst of it,
' and to what a height our senseless Heats
' and Animosities are since risen. God
' was pleased to take him away from that
' unpleasant sight, which would certainly
' have been as grievous to him as to any
' Man living.

' He never, that I know of, published
' any Thing in print, except only a Pre-
' face to that excellent Book of his learned
' Friend, Dr. *Cumberland*, of the Laws of
' Nature; partly perhaps out of Modesty,
' but chiefly I think out of Judgment: As
' deeming it best, when a Man is at his
' own Liberty, and urged thereto by no
' pressing Occasion, to defer the Business
          ' of

' of publick writing to the most mature
' and improved part of his Life; but what-
' ever his Reason was, it is not fit that
' those weighty and well digested Discour-
' ses which he left behind him should be
' suppressed, and the Publick defrauded of
' the Benefit and Advantage of them; and
' though they are only transcribed from his
' ordinary Sermon Notes, and want the
' exactness they would have had, if they
' had been designed and prepared for the
' Press by his own Hand, yet I think in
' the main they have the Perfection which
' he chiefly aimed at, in that they are very
' well fitted to do good, and to make
' those that read them wiser and bet-
' ter. For he thoroughly understood the
' Nature of Religion, the excellent De-
' sign, and the happy Effects of it, where
' it is sincerely embraced and entertain-
' ed; and he knew how to distinguish
' genuine and substantial Piety from that
' which is counterfeit and superficial. He
' had likewise a just and lively Sense of the
' mighty concernment and importance of
' Religion both to the private and publick,
' the present and future, the temporal and
' eternal Happiness of Men; which made
' him seek out all Sorts of Arguments to
' convince them of the absolute Necessity,
' and unspeakable Advantages of Religi-
' on, and all Kinds of Motives and In-
' ducements

' ducements to perfwade and allure them
' to the Practice of it; fo that by one Con-
' fideration or other he might take hold of
' all Capacities and Tempers of Men. But
' this will much better appear by a careful
' perufal of the Difcourfes themfelves, than
' by any laboured Commendation of them.

J. TILLOTSON.

Now let us view this Good Man in a
Scene of Friendfhip. In the Year 1687,
his intimate Acquaintance, Mr. NICHO-
LAS HUNT of *Canterbury*, lay dangeroufly
ill of a *Cancer*, and when Dr. TILLOTSON
was informed that he was paft Recovery,
he fent him the following excellent Letter
of Confolation, to comfort and fupport
him under the preffure of his lingring In-
difpofition.

S I R,

I AM *forry to underftand by Mr.* JANE-
WAY'S *Letter to my Son, that your Di-
ftemper grows upon you; and that you feem to
decline fo faft; I am very fenfible how much
eafier it is to give Advice againft Trouble in
the Cafe of another, than to take it in our
own.*

*It hath pleafed God to exercife me of late
with a very fore Trial, in the Lofs of my dear
and only Child, in which I do perfectly fubmit*

to

to his good Pleasure: firmly believing that he
always does that which is best; and yet, though
Reason be satisfied, our Passion is not so soon
appeas'd; and when Nature has received a
Wound, Time must be allowed for the Healing
of it. Since that, God hath thought fit to give
me a nearer Summons of a closer Warning of
my own Mortality, in the Danger of an Apo-
plexy; which yet, I thank God for it, hath
occasioned no very Melancholy Reflections;
but this perhaps is more owing to Natural Temper, than Philosophy and wise Considerations.

Your Case, I know, is very different, who
are of a Temper naturally melancholy, and under a Distemper apt to increase it; for both
which great Allowances ought to be made: And
yet methinks, both Reason and Religion do offer us Considerations of that Solidity and
Strength, as may very well support our Spirits
under all Frailties and Infirmities of the Flesh;
such as these;

That God is perfect Love and Goodness;
that we are not only his Creatures, but his
Children, and are as dear to him as to our
selves; that he does not afflict willingly, nor
grieve the Children of Men; and that all Evils
of Afflictions which befal us, are intended for
the Cure and Prevention of greater Evils of
Sin and Punishment; and therefore we ought
not only to submit to them with Patience, as being deserved by us; but to receive them with
Thankfulness, as being design'd by him to do
us

us that good, and to bring us to that Sense of him and our selves which nothing else perhaps would have done. That the Sufferings of this present Life are but short and light, compared with those extreme and endless Miseries which we have deserved; and with that exceeding Weight of Glory which we hope for in the other World, if we be careful to make the best Preparations for Death and Eternity. Whatever brings us nearer our End, brings us nearer to our Happiness; and how rugged soever the Way be, the Comfort is, that it leads us to our Father's House, where we shall want nothing we can wish for. Now we labour under a dangerous Distemper, which threatens our Life; what would we not be contented to bear, in order to a perfect Recovery, could we but be assured of it? and should we not be willing to endure much more, in order to Happiness, and that eternal Life which God that cannot lie hath promised? Nature, I know, is fond of Life, and apt to be still lingring after a longer Continuance here; and yet a long Life, with the usual Burthens and Infirmities of it, is seldom desirable; it is but the same things over again, or worse: So many more Nights and Days, Summers and Winters, a Repetition of the same Pleasures, but with less Pleasure and Relish; every Day a Return of the same, and greater Pains and Trouble; but with less Strength and Patience to bear them. These and the like Considerations I use to entertain my self withal, not only with Content-ment but Comfort; though with great Inequality of Temper at several Times, and with much Mixture of Human Frailties, which will always stick to us, while we are in this World: However, by these kind of Thoughts Death seems more familiar to us, and we shall be able by Degrees to bring our Minds close up to it, without starting at it. The greatest Tenderness I find in my self is with regard to some Relations; especially the dear and constant Companion of my Life, which I confess doth very sensibly touch me: But then I consider, and so, I hope, will they also, that this separation will be but a very little while; and that though I shall leave them in a bad World, yet under the Care of a good God, who can be more and better to them than all other Relations, and will certainly be so to those that love him, and hope in his Mercy.

I shall not need to advise you what to do, and what Use to make of this Time of your Visitation. I have Reason to believe, that you have been careful in the Time of your Health to prepare for the evil Day; and have been conversant in those Books which give the best Directions to this Purpose: And have not, as too many do, put off the great Work of your Life to the End of it: And then you have nothing to do, but as well as you can, under your present Weakness and Pains, to renew your Repentance for all the Errors and Miscarriages of

your

your Life; and earnestly to beg God's Pardon and Forgiveness of them, for his sake who is the Propitiation for our Sins: In comforting your self in the Goodness and the Promises of God, and the Hopes of that Happiness you are ready to enter into; and in the mean time, to exercise Faith and Patience for a little while; and be of good Courage, since you see Land; the Storm which you are in will soon be over, and then it will be as if it had never been; or rather the Remembrance of it will be a Pleasure.

I do not use to write such long Letters, but I do heartily compassionate your Case, and should be glad if I could suggest any thing that might help to mitigate your Trouble, and make the sharp and rugged Way through which you are to pass into a better World, a little more smooth and easy.

I pray God to fit us both for that great Change which we must once undergo; and if we be but in any good Measure fit, sooner or later makes no great Difference.

I commend you to the Father of Mercies, and the God of all Consolation; beseeching him to increase your Faith and Patience; and to stand by you in your last and great Conflict; that when you walk through the Valley of the Shadow of Death, you may fear no Evil; and when your Heart fails, and your Strength fails, you find him the Strength of your Heart, and your Portion for ever.

Farewell,

Farewell, my good Friend, and whilst we are here, let us pray for one another, that we may have a joyful Meeting in another World. So I rest,

Your truly affectionate
Friend and Servant,

J. TILLOTSON.

Mr. HUNT received this Letter with great Joy, and during his long Sickness behav'd himself with a truly Christian Fortitude; shortly after, it pleased God to remove him from this painful Life to that of Bliss and Immortality.

The succeeding Year brought on the late Glorious Revolution, in which Dr. TILLOTSON had too large a Share either to escape the Notice and Gratitude of those who conducted that great Affair, or to avoid the Calumny and Detraction of those who condemned both that Action and all its Approvers. It was his Happiness, that his Enemies, and those of the Government, were the same Persons; that none disliked him but who seem'd to act in Contradiction to Providence it self, disclaiming that very Blessing which they had pray'd and look'd earnestly for before. The Knowledge which the Doctor had of
the

the Scheme which the Patriots of their
Country had some time before the Revolution in view, is imputed to him as a
heavy Charge by his Adversaries; but to
hear that Objection from the Mouth of a
Church of England-Man, for whose Security chiefly that great Work was undertaken, is a Reproach highly unbecoming
the meanest of her Sons. The *Revolution*
found Dr. TILLOTSON *Dean* of *Canterbury*
and *Residentiary* of St. *Paul*'s, both eminent Stations in the Church, tho' inferior
to his Merit; yet was the Possessor humble enough to think them too considerable
for one Person. However he made the
best Use of them, their Revenues serving
only to enlarge his Capacity of doing good,
and giving him an Occasion to scatter the
Seeds of *Virtue* in more different Soils, by
which some at least might fall upon *good
Ground*, and multiply exceedingly. One,
who knew him perhaps as well as any Man,
assures us, that he neither slackened his
Labours, nor advanced his Fortunes by his
Preferments. He did not content himself
with such a *Residence* as answered the *Statute*; that was barely doing his Duty,
and only the Avoidance of Scandal, a
Pitch of Virtue too low for one who had
so just a Notion of Piety, and so lively a
Sense of the Force of Example. He gave
as much of his Time and Labours to his
Cathe-

Cathedral, as was consistent with his Obligation to Attendance on the Court. Neither when he was there, by the Necessity of his Duty (for he was the King's Chaplain) did he make that Use of a Court-Soil as is usual, but contented himself with deserving, not solliciting greater Preferments.

In the Year 1689, it was soon discover'd what Interest this Great *Man* might have made, if his Temper wou'd have allowed him, in the Court of *King WILLIAM* and *Queen MARY*, who were so fond and desirous of having him near them, to advise them, as well in the publick, as their own private Religious Concerns, that they gave him the Place of *Clerk* of the Closet, on purpose to oblige him to a more frequent resort to Court. These Princes, who had so happily preserved our endanger'd Religion, sought out for the best Means, and fittest Instruments to secure and establish it against any future Relapse; and as soon, therefore, as the Civil Liberties were a little settled, the Ecclesiastical came next under their Consideration. The powerful Interest of the Papists in the late Reign, had laid the poor Non-conformists under the Penalty of several severe Laws, which were accounted no small Dishonour to the Protestant Name: But now these being suspended by an Act of *Toleration;*

and

He is made Clerk of the Closet.

and a Chriftian Liberty indulged to Diffenters; fome who were not contented with
this favourable *Act* alone, ftrove to back
it with another, which was calculated to
take them all into the Bofom of the *Church*
of *England*. This Scheme was well known
by the Name of the COMPREHENSION,
of which fome were very fond, and others
wholly averfe to it; both Parties thinking
themfelves in the right, and actuated by
the true Spirit of Chriftianity, fell into very indecent, and unchriftian Treatment
of each other; the common, but fatal Effects of Attempts in Alterations of Religion. However, a Bill was brought in, and
paffed the Houfe of *Peers*, but when it
came to the *Commons* they defired his *Majefty* to fummon a *Convocation*, and lay the
Matter before them. And here the *Pa-
trons* and Sticklers for *Church Power*, would
do well to confider the Service Dr. TIL-
LOTSON did their Caufe upon this Occafion, and retract fome, at leaft, of the fevere Calumnies they have loaded his Memory with, as one who was no Friend to
his own Order, and bent upon abridging
it of its undoubted Privileges. What Notice we take of the Fact, as it is related by
Dr. NICHOLS, fhall not only be *Hiftorical*,
but, if poffible, fuch as may wipe off thefe
Afperfions; fuch Remarks having a fair
Connection to the *Life* of the Perfon which
we

we are relating. *First* then, take the Account of Dr. NICHOLS; * "Whilft this
" Bill was paffing, Dr. TILLOTSON, a
" Perfon of excellent Judgment, and then
" Clerk of the Clofet to the King, declared
" his Opinion againft it. And as he had a
" great Intereft in the King's Affections,
" fo he made ufe of it in bringing him o-
" ver to his Opinion in this Matter. He
" laid before him how frequently we had
" been reflected on by the Papifts, that
" our Reformation was founded chiefly
" upon Parliamentary Authority; that we
" fhould not give them a Handle for any
" fuch Objection for the future. That the
" Affairs of the Church did chiefly belong
" to Synodical Authority, and if they were
" paffed by the venerable Members of the
" Convocation, they would not only be
" more acceptable to the Body of the Clergy,
" but would be more religioufly obferved
" by the Laity. Adding, moreover, that
" leaft Affairs of this Nature, confifting of
" fuch a multitude of Particulars, might
" too flowly go on in fo numerous a Body;
" the beft way would be, as had formerly
" been done, to Commiffionate feveral of
" the moft Eminent of the Clergy to confi-

* Vid. *A Defence of the Doctrine and Difcipline of the
Church of England.* 12°. Page 115, 116, 117.

G 2   " der

" Men of some Methods how to heal the
" Wounds of the Church, and to establish
" a perpetual Peace among us. What they
" should agree upon, to be consider'd o-
" ver again by the more consummate Wis-
" dom of a Convocation: And what these
" should consent to, should be establish'd
" first by the Synodical, and afterwards by
" the Parliamentary Authority.

This was certainly very reasonable
Advice, and of no small Moment to the
Church, as it took off the Objection of a Parliamentary Religion, an Objection which
the *Papists* have urged with all their force
of Argument and Wit. I shall not consider
whether the *Roman Catholicks* way of Reasoning is just, it being sufficient to say,
that they imputed it as an high *Scandal* to
the *Church* of *England,* to owe its Settle-
ment to such a Hand; and therefore the
mitigation of that Scandal was wresting an
Arrow out of the Quiver of the Enemy, or
at least rendring it incapable of wounding
when it was thrown. Beside, that this
prudent Course which Dr. TILLOTSON advised, seemed the most probable of any to
take Effect, as not irritating the Spirits of
Men by lessening their Authority on either
Side, the Ecclesiastical and Civil Powers
being both preserved in their Rights, and
exercising their distinct Provinces by this
Method which he prescribed. How much

Con-

Controversy and Contention do we here see vanish into nothing! only by putting Business in the proper Channel it should flow in, which a less warm Head might have easily confounded, and got a Reputation too for doing either Party so considerable a Service, as engaging them in a Quarrel. But I believe I need not urge the wise Management of this worthy Person any farther, as an Argument of his Respect to the *Church*, or his tender Regard to her Authority. Dr. CALAMY * ; and sure the Words of an Enemy may be useful, says, *That it was a very bad piece of Advice*, and would insinuate to his Readers, as if the Adviser himself repented it afterwards. But till he can find a better Reason for it, than his bare Conjecture, we ought to believe, that the Man who was honest enough to give such good Counsel, had before considered the Matter so well, as to take care that it should never give him any other uneasiness, than what arose from its want of Success.

The *King*, in compliance to this Advice, summoned a Convocation, and issued out another Commission to *Thirty Divines* to prepare Matters to be laid before the Convocation, in this Affair of the COMPRE-

---

* Vid. *His Abridgment of Mr.* Baxter's *Life*, pag. 446.

pension. It may not be improper, considering the great Share Dr. TILLOTSON had in this Business, to insert the Commiffion in this Place, which is as follows:

The New Ecclefiaftical Commiffion.

     " WHEREAS the particular Forms
        " of Divine Worfhip, and the
" Rites and Ceremonies appointed to be u-
" fed therein, being Things in their own
" Nature indifferent and alterable, and fo
" acknowledg'd, it is but reafonable, that
" upon weighty and important Confidera-
" tions, according to the various exigencies
" of Times and Occafions, fuch Changes
" and Alterations fhould be made therein, as
" to thofe that are in Place and Authority,
" fhould from time to time feem either ne-
" ceffary or expedient.

     " And whereas the Book of Canons is
" fit to be reviewed, and made more fuita-
" ble to the State of the Church. And
" whereas there are Defects and Abufes in
" the Ecclefiaftical Courts and Jurifdicti-
" ons; and particularly, there is not fuffi-
" cient Provifion made for the removing
" of fcandalous Minifters, and for the re-
" forming of Manners either in Minifters
" or People; and whereas it is moft fit
" that there fhould be a ftrict Method
" prefcrib'd for the Examination of fuch
" Perfons as defire to be admitted into Ho-
" ly Orders, both as to their Learning and
" Manners.   " We

" We therefore, out of our Pious, and
" Princely Care for the good Order and
" Edification, and Unity of the Church of
" *England*, committed to our Charge and
" Care ; and for the reconciling, as much
" as is possible, of all Differences among
" our good Subjects ; and to take away all
" Occasion of the like for the future, have
" thought fit to authorize and impower
" you, *&c.* and any Nine of you, whereof
" Three to be Bishops, to meet from
" time to time, as often as shall be need-
" ful; and to prepare such Alterations of
" the Liturgy and Canons, and such Pro-
" posals for the Reformation of Ecclesiasti-
" cal Courts ; and to consider of such other
" Matters as in your Judgments may most
" conduce to the Ends above-mention'd.

Ten of the Commissioners were then Bi-
shops, *viz.* Dr. LAMPLUGH Arch-Bishop
of *York*, Dr. COMPTON, Dr. MEW, Dr.
LLOYD, Dr. SPRAT, Dr. SMITH, Sir Jo-
NATHAN TRELAWNY, Dr. BURNET, Dr.
HUMFREYS, and Dr. STRATFORD, who
were the Bishops of *London*, *Winchester*,
St. *Asaph*, *Rochester*, *Carlisle*, *Exeter*, *Salis-
bury*, *Bangor*, and *Chester.* Twenty other
Dignitaries were added to them ; as Dr.
STILLINGFLEET, Dr. PATRICK, Dr. TIL-
LOTSON, Dr. MEGGOT, Dr. SHARPE, Dr.
KIDDER, Dr. ALDRICH, Dr. JANE, Dr.

HALL,

HALL, Dr. BEAUMONT, Dr. MOUNTAGUE,
Dr. GOODMAN, Dr. BEVERIDGE, Dr. BATTE-
LY, Dr. ALSTON, Dr. TENNISON, Dr. SCOTT,
Dr. FOWLER, Dr. GROVE, and Dr. WIL-
LIAMS.

Dr. NICHOLS * thus proceeds, " The
" Reverend Perſons do now forthwith ap-
" ply themſelves to the Buſineſs which
" was laid before them, and begin their
" Work with a Review of the Common-
" Prayer Book. And firſt of all the *Ca-*
" *lendar* comes under Examination, from
" whence the Apocryphal Leſſons are ex-
" punged, and Chapters out of the Cano-
" nical Books are ſubſtituted to be read in
" their room. The Creed which is call'd
" *Athanaſius's,* becauſe it is found fault
" with by ſome Perſons by reaſon of the
" Damnatory Sentences, is permitted to
" be chang'd for the Apoſtles Creed at the
" diſcretion of the Miniſter. The *Collects*
" throughout the whole courſe of the Year
" are revis'd, moſt of them being made a-
" new, and render'd more ſuitable to the
" Epiſtles and Goſpels of the Day; and this
" with ſo much Elegance and Purity of
" Stile, with ſo much pious Force and Ar-
" dor, as nothing could tend more to ex-
" cite Devotion in the Minds of the Hearers,

---

* Vid. *Ut ſupra,* pag. 118. *& ſeq.*

" and

" and to raise up their Souls to God. They
" were first drawn up by Dr. SIMON PA-
" TRICK, who had an excellent Talent
" this way; Dr. GILBERT BURNET added
" a further Life and Force and Spirit to
" them; after this they underwent the
" exquisite Judgment of Dr. STILLING-
" FLEET; the last and finishing stroke being
" given to them by Dr. TILLOTSON, who
" polished over whatever was left rough in
" the Compositions, with his smooth Lan-
" guage and flowingness of his easie Elo-
" quence. They likewise agreed upon a
" new *Translation of the Psalms* to be read
" in the daily Service of the Church, more
" agreeable to the Original than the pre-
" sent is; which Province was assign'd to
" Dr. KIDDER, a Person excellently well
" versed in the Oriental Tongues. Some
" few Expressions and Words, which ly-
" ing scatter'd about the Liturgy, are
" found fault with by its Adversaries,
" were collected by Dr. TENNISON; such
" clear Expressions being substituted in
" their stead, as were not liable to be ex-
" cepted against by the most captious.
" There were some few other things pro-
" posed, but which were entirely to be
" referred to the Synod. *First* of all, that
" the *Cross in Baptism* should be in the E-
" lection of the Parents either to have it
" sign'd in the Childrens Foreheads, or o-
                                " mitted.

" mitted. Secondly, If any Nonconformist
" Minister should return to the Church,
" he was not, as the Custom is now, to
" undergo a new Ordination; but to be ad-
" mitted into the Church by a Conditional
" Ordination, like as we are wont to do in
" the Baptism of those Persons, of whom
" it is doubtful whether they are baptized
" or not, the Bishop's Hands being impo-
" sed on them, as was the Custom amongst
" the * Ancients, in receiving those Cler-
" gy into the Church who had been or-
" dain'd by Hereticks. Which was the
" Method used by + Arch-Bishop BRAM-
" HALL, Primate of Ireland, when he gave
" Visitation to any, who had received Pres-
" byterian Orders in the times of the late
" Confusion.

The Convocation, or English Synod, 1689.

" The Convocation soon after assembled,
" all the Clergy either avowedly or in their
" Minds highly approving or condemning
" what had been done by the Commiss-
" oners with relation to the Alterations.
" The greater part of the Clergy of the
" Convocation being displeased with those
" who had declared for the Alterations,
" were very earnest to make Dr. JANE,

---

* " Dionys. Alexand. apud Euseb. Hist. Eccl. Lib. 7.
" Cap. 2. Con. Nic. 1. Can. 8. Just. sive Author Resp. ad
" Orthodox. Resp. 18 Theod. Hist. Eccl. Lib. 1. Cap. 8.
+ " Vid. *Bishop* Bramhall's *Life before his Works.*

" the

" the *Regius* Professor of *Oxford*, Prolocu-
" tor of the Convocation. The rest being
" Persons of very great Esteem in the
" Church, gave their Votes for Dr. Til-
" lotson; But being over-power'd by
" Numbers, their Attempt in that Affair
" was but in vain.

" After this the King ordering the Con-
" vocation to attend him, he declares his
" Mind to them to this purpose: He gives
" them earnest Assurances of his Favour;
" and tells them how much it was his De-
" sire, that all his Subjects should live
" peaceably and lovingly one with another,
" and unite in one Manner of Worship:
" That to this end he had appointed Com-
" missioners to prepare, and lay before the
" Convocation such things as they thought
" fit should be alter'd: That he heartily
" wish'd a good Agreement among them,
" and that the Points in dispute might be
" handled with that mild and charitable
" Temper which becomes Ministers of the
" Gospel.

" But many of the Convocation-men had
" entertained an Opinion which was ne-
" ver to be eradicated out of their Minds,
" That by this Device of Alterations, a
" Design was laid to undermine the Church:
" That Episcopacy being already abolished
" in *Scotland*, there were now Attempts
" made against the same in *England*. That
" they

" they were afraid many of the Commif-
" fioners for the Alterations were embark-
" ed in the fame unwarrantable Project,
" or impofed upon by the Fallacies of de-
" figning Men. That the Diffenters, al-
" though out of the Church, were already
" very formidable Enemies to it, but if let
" into the Church they would overturn its
" Conftitution. That the Church was
" fufficiently protected by the Act of Uni-
" formity, which if once repealed, they
" knew not what the then prefent Parlia-
" ment, which they thought fhew'd too
" much Friendfhip to the Diffenters, might
" eftablifh in lieu thereof. That they had
" rather have what was prefent and fafe,
" than what was future and uncertain.

" The other Party pleaded thus, That
" the unhappy Contentions between the
" Nonconformifts and us had too long ra-
" ged: That now both of us being tired
" with quarelling, wifhed for Peace: That
" unlefs the Convocation did offer fome
" Terms of Accommodation, the Bifhops
" would not be able to juftifie themfelves,
" in making good what they had in the
" late Reign fo religioufly promifed. That
" it was underftood by all who fo highly
" approved their Propofitions, that they
" made this Offer of Reconcilation with
" the Diffenters, in the Name of all the
" Members of our Church, and therefore
                                    " it

" it would be an unworthy thing to pro-
" mise That, in the time of our Adversity,
" which in our Prosperity we should re-
" fuse to make good. That the King be-
" ing now earnestly bent upon this De-
" sign, would use all his Interest to pro-
" mote it; but if we should provoke him
" by making him undergo a Repulse in
" this Attempt, he wou'd not so easily be
" brought again to comply with it, when
" we our selves should desire it: That the
" King had ordered nothing to be laid be-
" fore the Parliament, but what should be
" before agreed to by the Convocation:
" That if the Parliament should design a-
" ny thing unkind to the Church, they
" might establish it by a secular Law for
" all that the Convocation could do to
" hinder it. And, *Lastly*, Tho' the Non-
" conformists should obstinately refuse to
" come into the Church upon the Con-
" cessions which were made for their sakes,
" yet nothing was laid before the Con-
" vocation but what would tend to the
" greater Honour of the Church: That
" by these Alterations the Constitution of
" the Church would be better'd, and all Pre-
" tence of Separation would be taken away.

" Disputes on both sides were carried on
" with great Eagerness, and at last the Sy-
" nod is dissolv'd, without concluding any
" thing. But no Misfortune so sensibly af-
" flicted

" flicted the Church, as this Diffension be-
" tween the Clergy. For hitherto our
" Clergy had lived with great Concord a-
" mong themselves, not to be divided by
" any Arts of their Adverfaries. For in
" the late Times, under their moft afflicted
" Condition, when they were turn'd out
" of, or fequeftred from, their Livings; by
" reafon of their good Correfpondence with
" one another, they bore their Afflictions
" the more eafily.   And afterwards, when
" their Condition was better'd, no Envy,
" which is wont to diffolve the Friendfhip
" of others, was able to interrupt their A-
" mity : But now, when all of them, per-
" haps, in their feveral ways, were defirous
" to promote the good of the Church, they
" unfortunately accufed each other for car-
" rying on Defigns for its Ruin." Thus far
Dr. NICHOLS.

In the Year 1691, after a long and pati-
ent Expectation on the fide of the Government, that the *Nonjuring Bifhops* would
comply to take the *Oaths*, which they at
laft abfolutely refufed, it was refolved to
deprive them, and fill up the vacant *Sees.*
Among thefe *Arch-Bifhop* SANCROFT was
one, whom no Overtures, nor Condefcen-
fions on the part of fome *great Reconcilers,*
could bring to acquiefce in the Conduct of
the *Revolution,* and take the *Oaths* to the
KING and QUEEN.   It is not to our purpofe

pose to examine into the Reasons of his
Refusal; a great, and good Man he surely
was, tho' without any disrespect to his Memory, we may say, far inferior to his Suc-
cessor Dr. TILLOTSON. He it was who *Made*
was pitched upon in these difficult times to *Arch-Bi-*
sit at the Head, and steer the *Church*. His *shop of*
natural Modesty made him earnestly at first, *Canterbu-*
withstand the Royal Favour, tho' he was *ry.*
at last prevail'd upon to accept of it; and
certainly a fitter Person in every Man's O-
pinion, but his own, could not be found.
It will not be improper to set down the
Words of a great Historian, which give
us both the Motives of his Refusal, and Ac-
ceptation of that high Dignity. ' He
' withstood it not (says the Bishop of
' *Salisbury* *) from any feeble, or fearful
' Considerations, relating to himself: He
' was not afraid of a Party, nor concern'd
' in such Censures and Calumnies as might
' be thrown upon him: He was not unwil-
' ling to sacrifice the Quiet of his Life,
' which he apprehended might soon de-
' cline and sink under so great a load. The
' Pomp of Greatness, the Attendance upon
' Courts, and a high Station, were indeed
' very contrary to his Genius: But tho'
' these were Grounds good enough to make

---

* *In his Funeral Sermon.*

' him

' him unwilling to rise higher in the World,
' yet none of them seem'd strong enough,
' to fix him to an obstinate Refusal. That
' which went the deepest in his own Mind,
' and which he laid out the most earnestly
' before their MAJESTIES, was, that those
' groundless Prejudices with which his E-
' nemies had loaded him, had been so in-
' dustriously propagated, while they were
' neglected by himself, that he believ'd,
' that he, who (as his Humility made him
' think) could at no time do any great Ser-
' vice, was less capable of it now than e-
' ver. But their MAJESTIES persisting in
' their Intentions, he thought it was the
' Voice and Call of God to him, and so he
' submitted : Yet with a heaviness of Mind
' that no Man knew better than my self.
' But as he engag'd in it, he form'd two
' settled Resolutions, from which he never
' departed. The one was, That whenso-
' ever the State of their MAJESTIES Af-
' fairs was such, that he could hope to be
' dismiss from that Post, he would become
' a most importunate Suitor to be deliver'd
' from it. The other was, That if the Infirmi-
' ties of Age should have so overtaken him
' that he could not go through the Fatigue
' and Labours of it, then he would hum-
' bly offer it up to their MAJESTIES : And
' he charg'd some of his most particular
' Friends to use all Freedom with him in
                          ' this

' this Matter, if they should obferve it,
' before it were perceiv'd by himfelf.'
Thus the Bifhop of *Salisbury*; and for my
own part, I think it unfair to fufpect an
Account given from *one* who had fo many
Opportunities of a right Information from
a perfonal Knowledge, and intimate Acquaintance with this Great Man. This
kind of *Holy Force*, if we may fo call it, had
been us'd in the Primitive Times to many
of the *Fathers*; nor was his Carriage lefs
humble, or his Conduct lefs glorious than
Theirs, in the fhort Scene which he acted
on this Stage. Confonant to this, fee that
moft excellent *Form of Prayer* * which he
compos'd on this Occafion, and the Prepa-
ration thereto, for that Great *Truft* with
which he was about to be invefted; take
in his own Words, *viz.*

' *May* 30, 1691. The Day before my
' Confecration to the Arch-Bifhoprick,
' which was on *Whitfunday* at St. *Mary le*
' *Bow*, when, on *Whitfunday* Eve I retir'd
' to *Edmonton*, to fpend that Day in Faft-
' ing and Prayer, to implore the Bleffing
' of Almighty God upon that Action, and
' the Affiftance of his Grace and Holy Spi-
' rit to be vouchfafed to his finful and

---

* *See the* 14*th Vol. of his Pofthumous Works,* pag. 104.
& feq.

H   un-

' unworthy Servant, whom his wife Pro-
' vidence, and the importunate Desire of
' their Majesties, King WILLIAM and
' Queen MARY, the best of *Princes*, (whom
' God in great Mercy to a most sinful and
' perverse People hath by a most signal
' Providence set upon the Throne of these
' Kingdoms, and sent (I trust) to be our
' Deliverers and Benefactors for many Ge-
' nerations yet to come) have call'd to the
' Government and Conduct of this mifer-
' ably distracted CHURCH in a very diffi-
' cult and dangerous Time.

' I began with a *short Prayer* to Almigh-
' ty God to prepare my Heart for the Du-
' ty of this Day, and to assist me in the
' Discharge of it, in such a manner as might
' be acceptable in his sight, thro' *Jesus*
' *Christ* my blessed Saviour and Redeemer.

' I proceeded next to a *Thanksgiving* to
' Almighty God for his Mercy and Good-
' ness to me in the Conduct of my whole
' Life, from my first Entrance into the
' World, to this Day.

' Next I made an humble and penitent
' *Confession* of my Sins, and earnest Sup-
' plication for the Pardon and Forgiveness
' of them.

' Next a *Prayer* for God's Blessing upon
' me, and his Holy Spirit to be conferr'd
' upon me, in the solemn *Dedication* of me
' the Day following to this High and Holy
' Office.   ' Then

' Then I read the Prayers in the *Confe-*
' *cration Office*.   I concluded with a Prayer
' for the KING and QUEEN, and a short
' Ejaculation.

! This his Behaviour, was, I think, truly *Primitive*, and a sure Presage of that
Peace and Tranquility the Church would
enjoy under so good a *Pastor*.   But no
sooner was he possess'd of this eminent
Station, than that restless *Party* who
had oppos'd all his former kind Offices
relating to the *Comprehension*, began to
murmur, and express their Resentments
at his Promotion ; but such Men gave him
no uneasiness : ' He being (says Dr. † NI-
' CHOLS) a Man of an extraordinary Pie-
' ty, and a great Lover of Peace ; and for
' fear that any Reflection should be cast
' upon our Religion, upon account of the
' Disagreement of the most considerable
' Men of the Church, upon the Contro-
' versie concerning *Alterations*, he did o-
' mit letting the *Convocation* sit for a confi-
' derable Time.   Neither was there any
' Man, at that Time, that was displeas'd
' at this long Recess of that *Body*.   They
' that were for *Alterations* did hope, that
' after a considerable Intermission, all
' Mens Passions would be so asswag'd,

---

† Vid. *Ut supra*, pag. 124, &c.

' that

' that they wou'd confent together in the
' fame Opinion. And thofe of the other
' *Party* were not difpleas'd, that thofe Mat-
' ters which they had not a liking to, were
' not again importunately urg'd upon
' them ; efpecially when the Occafion was
' taken away, of being oblig'd to reject
' what was propos'd to them by their
' PRINCE, and that they were not neceffi-
' tated to incur the Difpleafure of their
' prefent Arch-Bifhop.' *Thus (fays the*
Bifhop of Salisbury) he went on, while
his Enemies were ftill endeavouring to bear
down a Reputation, which gave him, as they
thought, too great an Authority.

In the Year 1693. the Arch-Bifhop met
with a Difficulty in the exercife of his *Vi-*
fitatorial Power, concerning which, all the
Light we can collect, is from a Manufcript
communicated by that learned Antiquary,
Mr. THORESBY of *Leeds.* It was a *Cafe*
between the *Warden* and *Fellows* of *All-*
Souls College in *Oxford* on one fide, and
one Mr. PROAST, a *Chaplain* of theirs,
whom they had remov'd, on the other,
and who had appeal'd to the *Arch-Bifhop.*
We may fee there a Specimen of this good
Man's compofing Temper, by the Courfe
he advifed in this Affair, by which both
Parties preferved their *Rights,* and the
Peace of the *Society* was reftored. The
Manufcript is as follows.

May

May it pleafe your GRACE,

'A Fter we had received your GRACE's
' 'Order, in which you was plea-
' fed to give the *College of All-Souls* time till'
' the 15th of *November*, to endeavour to
' compofe the Differences between the
' Honourable Mr. FINCH our *Warden*,
' and Mr. PROAST, within a few Days
' we had a Letter from our *Warden*, ex-
' horting us to proceed according to your
' GRACE's Order, and promifing to com-
' ply with any Conditions we fhould pro-
' pofe, as juft and equitable to him, or as
' kind to Mr. PROAST.

' Upon this we delegated the five Offi-
' cers, and the five Seniors of the Col-
' lege, to receive the Propofals of the dif-
' agreeing Parties, to confider and report
' their Opinion to the College, in order to
' lay the whole Proceeding before your
' GRACE. Thefe Delegates met, and
' Mr. PROAST deliver'd to them a Paper
' containing thefe following Articles.

1. ' *As to the Difgrace of my pretended*
' *Expulfion, the unworthy Practices which*
' *have been ufed to confirm it; the Toil of fo*
' *many Journeys as I have been forc'd to*
' *take, to get it annull'd; and all the reft of*
' *the Trouble and Vexation which hath been*
' *given me for thefe Things, I expect no a-*
' *mends, but am ready to forgive them, only*

H 3   ' re-

‘ reserving to my self a Right to vindicate my
‘ good Name, as I shall find it necessary, a-
‘ gainst the Calumnies and Aspersions, by
‘ which some have endeavoured to deprive me
‘ of that also. But the Things which I con-
‘ ceive I have reason to desire and expect, are
‘ these that follow, viz.

2. ‘ That I be restored to the Possession of
‘ my Place, with all the Profits belonging to it,
‘ for the Time that I have stood dispossess'd of it.

3. ‘ That I be reimbursed the Expences I
‘ have been put to in seeking to recover it.

4. ‘ That the Order made December 8,
‘ 1688. that I should be desired to forbear co-
‘ ming to the College Chappel, be expunged out
‘ of the Register of the College: And that it
‘ be own'd and declared by the Society in the
‘ said Register, that the Chaplains of the Col-
‘ lege are not subject to be depriv'd of their
‘ Places, or to be any other Ways punished by
‘ the Warden alone, or by any less Authority
‘ than that by which the Scholars and Fellows
‘ are to be depriv'd, or otherwise punish'd;
‘ and that in case of unjust Deprivation, or
‘ any other Grievance, they have an undoubted
‘ Right to seek Redress, by appealing to the Vi-
‘ sitor of the College.

‘ This Paper the Delegates transmitted
‘ to the Warden, and receiving an An-
‘ swer that he would comply with any just
‘ and equitable Demands, but could not
‘ think these to be such, unless Mr. PROAST
                                                  pro-

' produced better Reafons than he could
' ever yet meet with. The Delegates de-
' fired Mr. PROAST to fhew his Demands
' to be reafonable and juft: But this he pe-
' remptorily refufed to do ; and being told
' that fuch a refufal tended to obftruct
' that Accommodation which our moft
' Reverend *Vifitor*'s Order engaged us to
' endeavour after, Mr. PROAST reply'd
' with fome fiercenefs, *I defire Juftice, not*
' *Accommodation*; and being again told,
' we would endeavour to do him all the
' Juftice we could, and even according to
' his own Demands, if he could fhew
' them to be reafonable and juft; he re-
' peated his former Words, and fo left us.

' However, the *Delegates* conceiving
' themfelves obliged by your GRACE's
' Order to endeavour to compofe the Dif-
' ference between the *Warden* and Mr.
' PROAST, did with great Care and Ap-
' plication confider the *Statutes of the Col-*
' *lege*, and after Deliberation upon, and
' Debates concerning them, unanimoufly
' agreed to return thefe following Anfwers
' to Mr. PROAST's Paper.

' To your firft Demand, in which you
' require *to be reftor'd to the Poffeffion*, &c.
' We return,

' That we cannot by any means defire
' the *Warden* to reftore you, becaufe you
' muft ground that Demand, as appears

' by your Fourth Article, upon thefe
' Words, *The Warden alone hath not Power*
' *to punifh or difpoffefs a Chaplain.* Where-
' as by the whole Tenor of our *Statutes* it
' is notorioufly evident, *That the Warden*
' *alone hath the Power to put in, govern,*
' *punifh, and difplace a Chaplain;* fo that
' without doing a great Injury to the *War-*
' *den,* and invading his Right, we cannot
' agree with you in that Demand, or make
' any Application to the *Warden* to com-
' ply with it.

' To the Second, in which you require
' *to be reimburs'd,* &c. We Anfwer, that
' you being difplac'd by our *Warden,*
' whom we acknowledge to have, and
' who undoubtedly hath Power to difplace
' you, we cannot make any Application to
' the *Warden* to reimburfe you any of
' thofe Expences you mention.

' To your Third Demand, in which you
' require, *That it be own'd and declar'd by*
' *the Society,* &c. We reply,

' That the Society can make no Decla-
' ration againft the Statutes of the College,
' and that the *Statutes* are in many Places
' *directly oppofite* to this unreafonable De-
' mand. And you may be affured that
' the *Fellows* of the College will be as care-
' ful to hinder all Encroachments upon
' their real Rights, as you can be to main-
' tain and fecure thofe fancy'd ones of
' *Chaplains.*   ' Thefe

' These Answers we make to your De-
' mands; and as for your forgiving Arti-
' cle, we thank you for it; and to shew
' you how sensible we are of your great
' Favours, we will endeavour to make a
' suitable return; and therefore all the un-
' worthy Practices that have been used to
' re-possess you of your Place; all the Scan-
' dal we have lain under by your frequent
' and publick charging many of us with
' Perjury, and particularly by that vile
' Calumny, when you publickly said be-
' fore our most Reverend Visitor, that the
' Petition lately presented to his GRACE,
' was clandestinely and surreptitiously ob-
' tain'd, together with a great many Things
' of that Nature, we are willing to forget,
' and heartily forgive.

' And farther, to make it evident that
' we do not act as *Parties* in this Cause,
' but with the greatest Kindness that any
' honest Men in our Circumstances can
' show to you, we do promise, upon your
' Declaration to live peaceably and quietly
' amongst us, and to be content with those
' Rights and Privileges which the *Statutes*
' *allow a Chaplain*, to desire the Warden to
' put you into a Place of *Chaplain*, and we
' do not doubt but he will comply with
' our Request.

' To this Paper, Mr. PROAST, after he
' had, as he said, considered it, answered,

' He

' *He return'd the Pardon that was in it,* (it
' being, it seems, more uneasy to some
' Men to receive, than to need a Pardon)
' *and was resolv'd to wait upon your* GRACE
' *the 15th of November.*

' But not then refusing the Kindness of-
' fer'd him in the last Article, the Delegates
' reported their Proceedings, together with
' their Opinion as to the Point, and the So-
' ciety agreed to request the *Warden* to
' put Mr. PROAST into a *Chaplain's* Place,
' there being one at that Time vacant:
' To this Request the *Warden* hath yield-
' ed, and Mr. PROAST is now *Chaplain* of
' *All-Souls College.*

' To this plain Narrative we beg leave
' to subjoin those Reasons that moved the
' Delegates to make the forementioned
' Answer to the Demands of Mr. PROAST.

' That the *Warden* alone hath Power, to
' put in a *Chaplain,* they were convinced
' by these Words in the Statute, *De totali*
' *numero Sociorum,* &c. *Non procurabo dimi-*
' *nutionem, mutationem, translationem, seu*
' *annullationem alicujus numeri, in aliquâ*
' *scientiâ, seu facultate, nec etiam numeri*
' *Presbyterorum, Clericorum, aut cæterorum*
' *Ministrorum capellæ dicti Collegii.* The
' like Obligation lying upon no Man but
' the *Warden,* for the *Fellows,* who are the
' only Persons beside the *Warden* who have
' an Interest in any Election relating to the
' Col-

' College of *All-Souls*, are obliged by theſe
' Words only: *Non procurabo diminutio-*
' *nem, tranſlationem, mutationem, ſeu an-*
' *nullationem alicujus numeri in aliquâ ſcientiâ*
' *ſeu facultate: Statutum de modo & formâ*
' *eligendi Scholares.* And it is notoriouſly
' evident, that the *Warden* alone hath no-
' minated every Chaplain ſince the Death
' of our good *Founder* *, and Mr. PROAST
' himſelf never had any Right, but what
' the ſingle Nomination of the then *War-*
' *den* gave him.

' That the *Warden* alone hath Power
' to govern, puniſh, and diſplace, a *Chap-*
' *lain*, they were perſwaded by theſe fol-
' lowing Clauſes: *In Stat. de totali numero*
' *Sociorum,* &c. *Semper unus ſit qui omnibus &*
' *ſingulis ejuſdem Collegii ſociis & Scholaribus,*
' *nec non Sacerdotibus, & miniſtris, aliiſq;*
' *quibuſcunque in eodem Coll. degentibus præ-*
' *emineat atque præſit, eoſdem ſecundum regu-*
' *las, & Statuta inferius edita, & in poſterum*
' *per nos, & Succeſſores noſtros Cantuar. Ar-*
' *chiepiſcopos edenda, ſtatutis & ordinationi-*
' *bus noſtris non contraria, nec aliquo modo*
' *repugnantia, regat, corrigat, & gubernat,*
' *qui perpetuus ſit, & cuſtos ejuſdem Collegii,*
' *vulgariter* Wardeyn *perpetuo nuncupetur.*
' *Stat. de officio Cuſtodis. Cuſtos omnibus*

---

* *Arch-Biſhop* Chiſheley.

' &

' *& singulis Scholaribus sociis, ministris Al-*
' *taris, Capellanis,* viz. *Et Clericis in dicti*
' *Collegii capellâ in divinis ministrare deben-*
' *tibus præmineat atque præsit, eosque juxta*
' *ordinationes & statuta dicti Collegii regat,*
' *dirigat, & gubernat.* The *Sub-Warden,*
' who is an Officer appointed by Statute
' in the Room of the *Warden* when absent,
' is entrusted with the same Power, and
' over the same Persons, *Stat. de Vice Custo-*
' *do: Vice Castos circa curam, &c. Scholari-*
' *um & Sociorum ipsius Collegii nec non mini-*
' *strorum in capellâ ejusdem Coll. in divinis*
' *ministrare debentium, vices ipsius Custodis*
' *ipso absente suppleat diligenter.*

' This is again confirm'd, *Stat. in qui-*
' *bus socii & Scholares,* &c. *Scholares, socii &*
' *personæ ac officiarii, & ministri dicti Coll.*
' *quicunque Custodi, & eo absente, Vice Cu-*
' *stodi in licitis & honestis obediant.*

From these several Clauses they were
' convinc'd the *Warden* hath Power to
' govern, punish, displace, *&c.* and that
' he alone hath Power, they concluded,
' because the Statutes joyn no Officer with
' the *Warden,* and give the *Deans* Power
' over none but *Scholars and Fellows. Stat.*
' *de Decanorum electione: Decani sub Custode*
' *Scholarium* (those who are in their Proba-
' tion Year; *Stat. de modo formâ eligendi*
' *Scholares) & Sociorum curam & regimen*
' *habeant.* And tho' the *Sub-Warden* is

' en-

' entrufted with the Government of thofe
' that are called *miniftri capellæ (Chaplains)*
' as well as the Government of the Scholars
' and Fellows, yet the Dean is then only
' to be joined with him, when Scholars or
' Fellows are to be punifh'd for their Faults.
' *Vice Cuftos poffit etiam præfente Cuftode Scho-*
' *lares & focios negligentes cum concenfu De-*
' *cani facultatis feu fcientiæ delinquentis cor-*
' *rigere.* Stat. de Vice Cuftode.

' Agreeable to thefe, is the *Stat. de Le-*
' *ctura Bibl. Lectura, focii Scholares ac ca-*
' *pellani fub filentio diligenter intendant;*
' then it follows, *Si quenquam Scholarium*
' *vel Sociorum in præmiffis reum contigerit re-*
' *periri, puneatur per Cuftodem, aut eo abfente*
' *Vice Cuftodem, & Decanum fuæ facultatis:*
' And in the Statute *de difpofitione camera-*
' *rum,* the Provifion for the Chaplains is
' left to the Difcretion of the Warden, *Cæ-*
' *teris vero cameris dicti Coll. ad ufum capella-*
' *norum, choriftarum, & fervientium ejuf-*
' *dem juxta arbitrium Cuftodis difponendum*
' *refervatis.* Nor could they find any one
' Claufe in the Statutes, which might fo
' much as feem to favour the contrary
' Opinion, unlefs that in the *Stat. de Suf-*
' *fragiis & Orat. Sociorum, Scholarium &*
' *capellanorum dicti Coll. noftri, &c. Siquis*
' *in prædictis pluries deliquerit, juxta arbi-*
' *trium Cuftodis & Decani fui vel Vice Cufto-*
' *dis & Decani prædicti acrius puniatur.* But
' this

' this Appearance of an Argument va-
' nish'd as soon as they had confidered,
' that this Clause would not agree with
' the Clauses of several other Statutes, un-
' lefs it were underftood diftributively,
' and the feveral Officers appointed by this
' Statute to punifh the feveral Delinquents,
' inflicted Punifhments upon thofe refpe-
' ctive Perfons, whom other Statutes had
' appointed them to correct and punifh;
' and that the Clause muft be thus under-
' ftood, they were fully perfwaded when
' they had farther confider'd, that a *Chap-*
' *lain* cannot be of any Faculty, and that
' he cannot have any Dean in *All Souls*
' College, as is notorioufly evident from
' the whole Tenor of our Statutes.

' The Anfwer to the firft Demand being
' thus fettled, we humbly conceive the
' other Two muft be good and fatisfactory,
' becaufe they naturally depend and follow
' upon this; and therefore we fhall only
' beg leave, farther to reprefent to your
' GRACE, our Carriage in this Proceeding.
' It was carry'd on with all the Calmnefs
' and Moderation poffible; there were no
' Heats, or intemperate Words amongft
' our felves, and not fo much as one rough
' or angry Expreffion ufed to Mr. PROAST,
' notwithftanding his rude, unmannerly
' Reflections on our *Warden*, and many
' Provocations both without Doors, and
' in

'in the College; and we hope it will ap-
'pear to your GRACE that we have all a-
'long acted with much more ingenuity
'and Temper, than that Man who fo
'fiercely clamour'd againft Accommoda-
'tion. We are

Your GRACE'*s most humble*
and dutiful Servants,
the College of All-Souls.

All-Souls,
Nov. 11th. 1693.

Mr. THORESBY acquaints us, that he
found the *College* unwilling to have this
Cafe publifhed, or to confent to give any
further infight into the Matter; but their
defires, for many Reafons, could not be
complied with; and it is their own fault
that we cannot give a fuller Account than
what this Manufcript affords.

The fame Year, (1693,) his GRACE pub- *He pub-*
lifh'd Four (incomparable) SERMONS *Con-* *lifhes Four*
cerning the Divinity *and* Incarnation *of our* *Sermons.*
Bleffed Saviour. *The true Reafon whereof,*
(*the Reader* is told in a fhort *Advertisement*
before them) *was not that which is commonly*
alledged for printing Books, the Importunity
of Friends ; *but the importunate Clamours*
and Calumnies *of* others, *whom the* Author
heartily prays God *to forgive, and to give*
them better minds : And to grant that the en-
fuing Difcourfes, the Publication *whereof was*
in fo great a degree neceffary, may by his Blef-
fing prove in fome meafure ufeful.

But

But among the Inconveniences which he expected in the due Discharge of this difficult Office, he found one Advantage, which was his Retirement from that Multitude of Labours, which either his neceſſary Buſineſs, or his Friendſhips poured in upon him. This left him at leiſure to bend his Thoughts towards the *Good* of the whole CHURCH, ſometimes himſelf propoſing uſeful Deſigns for it, ſometimes encouraging thoſe of others, and always praying for its *Proſperity*. To this End he, who liv'd but for the good of others, began to chuſe out ſome more of his excellent SERMONS, ſuch as he thought were the beſt calculated for the univerſal Promotion of Virtue and Piety. Theſe he eſpecially directed for inculcating the Principles of *Early Religion*, *Family Duties*, and *The Education of Children*. Conſiderations of the moſt extenſive and neceſſary Influence on the Minds and Lives of Mankind. See how the good Biſhop ſpeaks of them in the Tenderneſs of a Fatherly and Primitive Spirit, in the following *Preface*, which certainly breaths the Soul of that incomparable Man.

Publiſhes Six more Sermons in 1664.

' BEING, I hope, for the remainder
' of my Life, releaſed from that
' irkſome and unpleaſant Work of *Contro-*
' *verſy* and *Wrangling* about Religion, I
' ſhall now turn my Thoughts to ſome-
' thing

' thing more agreeable to my Temper,
' and of a more direct and immediate
' Tendency to the promoting of true Re-
' ligion, to the Happineſs of Human So-
' ciety, and the Reformation of the World.

' I have no Intention to reflect upon a-
' ny that ſtand up in Defence of the *Truth*,
' and contend earneſtly for it, endeavouring
' *in the Spirit of Meekneſs* to reclaim thoſe
' that are in *Error*. For I doubt not but
' a very good Man may upon ſeveral Oc-
' caſions be almoſt unavoidably engag'd in
' *Controverſies* of Religion ; and if he have
' a Head clear and cool enough, ſo as to be
' maſter of his own *Notions* and *Temper* in
' that hot kind of Service, he may therein
' do conſiderable Advantage to the *Truth*.
' Though a Man that hath once *drawn*
' *Blood in Controverſy*, as Mr. *Mede* expreſ-
' ſeth it, is ſeldom known ever perfectly
' to recover his own good Temper after-
' wards.

' For this Reaſon a good Man ſhould
' not be very willing, *when his Lord comes*,
' to *be found ſo doing*, and as it were *beat-*
' *ing his fellow Servants* : And all *Contro-*
' *verſy*, as it is uſually managed, is little
' better. A good Man would be loth to
' be taken out of the World reeking hot,
' from a ſharp Contention with a perverſe
' Adverſary ; and not a little out of Coun-
' tenance, to find himſelf in this Temper

I   ' tranſ-

' tranflated into the calm and peaceable *Re-*
' *gions* of the *Bleffed*, where nothing but
' perfect *Charity* and *good Will* reign for
' ever.

' ' I know not whether St. *Paul*, who had
' been *taken up into the third Heavens*, did
' by that Queftion of his, *Where is the Dif-*
' *pater of THIS WORLD?* intend to in-
' finuate, that this *wrangling* Work hath
' Place only in *this World*, and upon this
' *Earth*, where *only* there is a *Duft* to be
' raifed; but will have no Place in the *o-*
' *ther*. But whether St. *Paul* intended this
' or not, the Thing it felf I think is true,
' that in the *other World* all Things will be
' clear and paft *Difpute*. To be fure, a-
' mong the *Bleffed*; and probably alfo a-
' mong the *Miferable*, unlefs fierce and fu-
' rious Contentions, with great *Heat* with-
' out *Light*, about Things of no moment
' and concernment to them, fhould be de-
' fign'd for a part of their *Torment*.

' As to the following *Sermons*, I am fen-
' fible that the *Style* of them is more loofe
' and full of Words, than is agreeable to
' juft and exact *Difcourfes*: But fo I think
' the *Style* of *Popular Sermons* ought to be.
' And therefore I have not been very care-
' ful to mend this Matter; chufing rather
' that they fhould appear in that native
' Simplicity in which, fo many Years ago,
' they were firft fram'd, than drefs'd up
' with

' with too much Care and Art. As they
' are, I hope the candid and ingenuous
' Readers will take them in good part.

' And I do heartily wish that all that
' are concern'd in the respective *Duties*,
' treated on in the following *Sermons*,
' would be persuaded so to lay them to
' Heart, as to put them effectually in
' Practice: That how much soever the
' Reformation of this corrupt and dege-
' nerate Age in which we live is almost ut-
' terly to be despair'd of, we may yet have
' a more comfortable prospect of future
' Times, by seeing the Foundation of a
' better World begun to be laid in the care-
' ful and conscientious Discharge of the
' Duties here mention'd: That by this
' means *the Generations to come may know*
' *God, and the Children yet unborn may fear*
' *the Lord.*

' I have great Reason to be sensible
' how fast the Infirmities of Age are com-
' ing upon me, and therefore *must work the*
' *Works of Him*, whose Providence hath
' placed me in the *Station* wherein I am,
' *whilst it is Day, because the Night cometh*
' *when no Man can work.*

' I knew very well, before I enter'd up-
' on this great and weighty *Charge*, my
' own manifold Defects, and how un-
' equal my best Abilities were for the due
' Discharge of it; but I did not feel this
I 2 ' so

‘ fo fenfibly as I now do every Day more
‘ and more. And therefore that I might
‘ make fome fmall amends for greater
‘ Failings, I knew not how better to
‘ place the broken Hours I had to fpare
‘ from almoft perpetual Bufinefs of one
‘ kind or other, than in preparing fome-
‘ thing for the Publick that might be of
‘ ufe to recover the decayed Piety and
‘ Virtue of the prefent Age; in which
‘ Iniquity doth fo much abound, and the
‘ Love of God and Religion is grown fo
‘ cold.

‘ To this end I have chofen to publifh
‘ thefe plain Sermons, and to recommend
‘ them to the ferious perufal, and faithful
‘ practice both of the *Paftors* and *People*
‘ committed to my Charge; earneftly be-
‘ feeching Almighty God, that by his Blef-
‘ fing they may prove effectual to that
‘ good End for which they are fincerely de-
‘ fign’d.

I need not relate the good Effects of
thefe, or any other of his Grace’s excellent
Compofitions, they were vifible in that
eager Thirft the World had after them;
and if well Watering the Flock be one great
Duty in the *Shepherd*, never did any *Paftor*
perform it better. Yet in the midft of thefe
good Works he could not efcape the Envy
and Malice of Men; and it were eafie to
gather

gather a plentiful Bundle of their Invectives,
if we thought such an Entertainment fit to
be transmitted to Posterity. But they are
dead, some in their Authors, some in their
malignant Pens, and all in the Memory of
good Men. It will be enough to touch.
upon them generally, in the Words of one
* we have often been oblig'd to quote,
‘ How false soever these Calumnies were
‘ generally known to be, the Confidence
‘ with which they were aver'd, join'd with
‘ the Envy that accompanies a high Stati-
‘ on, had a greater Operation than could
‘ have been imagin'd, considering how
‘ long he had liv'd on so publick a Scene,
‘ and how well he was known. It seem'd
‘ a new and unusual Thing, that a Man
‘ who in a Course of above Thirty Years
‘ had done so much Good, so many Servi-
‘ ces to so many Persons, without ever once
‘ doing an ill Office, or a hard Thing to a-
‘ ny one Person, who had a Sweetness and
‘ Gentleness in him, that seem'd rather to
‘ lean to Excefs, should yet meet with so
‘ much unkindness and injustice. But the
‘ returns of Impudence and Malice which
‘ were made to the *Son of God* himself,
‘ and to his *Apostles*, taught him to bear
‘ all this with Submission to the Will of

---

* *The Bishop of* Salisbury.

I 3   ‘ God;

' God; praying for those who despitefully
' us'd him, and upon all Occasions doing
' them Good for Evil. Nor had this any
' other effect on him, either to change his
' Temper or his Maxims, tho' perhaps it
' might sink too much into him, with rela-
' tion to his Health. He was so exactly
' true in all his Representations of Things
' or Persons, that he laid before Their MA-
' JESTIES, that he neither rais'd the Cha-
' racter of his Friends, nor sunk that of
' those who deserv'd not so well of him (I
' love not to say Enemies) but offer'd every
' Thing to them with that Sincerity that
' did so well become Him, that Truth and
' Candor was almost perceptible in every
' thing he said or did: His Looks and
' whole Manner seem'd to take away all
' Suspicion concerning him. For he thought
' nothing in this World was worth much
' Art, or great Management. With all
' these Things he strugled, till at last they
' overcame him, or rather he overcame
' them, and escaped from them.' For on
the 17th Day of *November*, in the Year
1694. he was siezed with a sudden Illness,
which proved Fatal to him, and mournful
to all the Friends of true Piety. The first
Attacks came upon him while he was in
that Employment in which he delighted
most, at Church, and in the Worship of
God: He bore them with his usual neglect

lect of himself: And tho' his Countenance
shewed he was ill, he would neither interrupt nor break off from those Sacred Ex-
ercises, nor make haft to look after his
Health.   Ah the unhappy Neglect! of a
Life that deserv'd so well to be carefully
preserv'd.   The Fit came on slowly, but
seem'd to be fatal.   All Symptoms were
Melancholy.   It soon turn'd to a *dead Pal-*
sie.   The Oppression was so great, that it
became very uneasie for him to speak, but
it appear'd that his Understanding was still
clear, tho' others could not have the Advantage of it: He only said, *That he had no*
Burden on his Conscience.   All Remedies
prov'd ineffectual: He expres'd no Concern to Live, nor Fear to Die; but patiently bore his Burden, till it sunk him on the
fifth Day, and in the Sixty fifth Year of
his Age.   Thus he Lived and thus he Died.
He was buried on the 30th of the same
Month, in the *Church* of St. *Lawrence Jewry,*
the *Bishop of Salisbury preaching* his *Funeral*
Sermon, taking for his Text St. *Paul's Epi-*
stle to *Tim.* Chap. IV. ver. 1. *I have fought*
the good Fight, I have finished my Course, I
have kept the Faith.   In his Discourse, tho'
from the natural Talents of the *Preacher,*
which were very great, and the intimacy
of their Friendship, of which none had a
greater share, one might reasonably expect
Justice to the Memory of the deceased; yet

was it such a Subject that even *Bishop*
Burnett could not himself reach in all
its Views, and describe with an adequate
Eloquence. He has said indeed a great
deal, and his Enemies have thought a great
deal too much, for they have rail'd themselves quite out of Temper upon this *Fune-*
ral Sermon. The *Non-juring* Clan attacked
both the Living and the Dead, in a Book
entituled, *Some Discourses upon Dr.* Burnett and Dr. Tillotson, *&c.* said to be
written by Mr. Lesley. To which the
Bishop reply'd in a judicious Defence * removing all the heap of Scandal they had
laid both on his Friend, and himself. The
Reader will be a better Judge how little
both of them deserved so scurrilous a
Treatment, by seeing what the *One* has
said of the *Other*, which can only be call'd
a just, decent, and modest Character of
his departed Friend; speaking of his early
Candor and Moderation towards those
Persons who differ'd from him, he did not
(says his *Lordship*) ' treat them with Con-
' tempt and Hatred, and he disliked all
' Levities and Railings upon those Sub-
' jects. This gave him great Advantages
' in dealing with them, and he still persist-
' ed in it, how much soever it was either

---

* See *the Bishop of* Salisbury's *Reflections on that Pamphlet,*
8v⁰. *printed* Anno 1696.

' disliked

' disliked or suspected by angry Men. As
' he got into a true Method of Study, so
' he entred into Friendships with some
' great Men, which contributed not a lit-
' tle to the perfecting his own Mind. There
' was then a Set of as extraordinary Per-
' sons, in the *University* where he was form-
' ed, as perhaps any Age has produced;
' they had clear Thoughts, and a vast
' Compass; great Minds, and Noble Tem-
' pers. But that which gave him his last
' finishing, was his close and long Friend-
' ship with Bishop WILKINS. He went
' into all the best Things that were in that
' Great Man, but so, that he perfected e-
' very one of them: For though Bishop
' WILKINS was the more Universal Man,
' yet *He* was the greater Divine: If the *one*
' had more Flame, the *other* was more
' Correct. Both acted with great Plain-
' ness, and were raised above regarding
' vulgar Censures. But if Bishop WIL-
' KINS had a Talent so peculiar to himself,
' that perhaps never Man could admonish
' and reprove with such Weight and Au-
' thority, and in a Way so obliging as he
' did; so no Man knew better than this
' his great Friend, the Art of gaining up-
' on Mens Hearts, and of making them-
' selves find out that which might be amiss
' in them, though the Gentleness and Mo-
' desty of his Temper had not so well
                              ' fitted

' fitted him for the rough Work of Re-
' proving.

' Having dedicated himself to the Ser-
' vice of the Church, and being sensible
' of the great Good that might be done by
' a plain and edifying Way of Preaching,
' he was very little disposed to follow the
' Patterns then set him, or indeed those of
' former Times. And so he set a Pattern
' to himself, and such an one it was, that
' 'tis hoped it will be long and much fol-
' lowed. He begun with a deep and close
' Study of the Scriptures, upon which he
' spent four or five Years, till he had arri-
' ved at a true Understanding of them.
' He studied next all the ancient Philoso-
' phers and Books of Morality: Among the
' Fathers St. BASIL and St. CHRYSOSTOM
' were those he chiefly read. Upon these
' Preparations he set himself to compose
' the greatest Variety of Sermons, and on
' the best Subjects, that perhaps any one
' Man has ever yet done. His joining
' with Bishop WILKINS in pursuing the
' Scheme of an *Universal Character,* led
' him to consider exactly the Truth of Lan-
' guage and Stile, in which no Man was
' happier, and knew better the Art of pre-
' serving the Majesty of Things under a
' Simplicity of Words; tempering these
' so equally together, that neither did his
' Thoughts sink, nor his Stile swell: Keep-
' ing

' ing always the due Mean between a low
' Flatnefs and the Dreffes of falfe *Rhetorick*:
' Together with the Pomp of Words he
' did alfo cut off all Superfluities and need-
' lefs Enlargements: He faid what was
' juft neceffary to give clear *Ideas* of Things,
' and no more: He laid afide all long and
' affected Periods: His Sentences were fhort
' and clear ; and the whole Thread was of
' a piece, plain and diftinct. No Affecta-
' tions of Learning, no fqueezing of Texts,
' no fuperficial Strains, no falfe Thoughts
' nor bold Flights, all was folid and yet
' lively, and grave as well as fine : So that
' few ever heard him, but they found fome
' new Thought occurred ; fomething that
' either they had not confidered before, or
' at leaft fo diftinctly, and with fo clear a
' View as he gave them.

   ' Whether he explained Points of Divi-
' nity, Matters of Controverfy, or the
' Rules of Morality, on which he dwelt
' moft copioufly, there was fomething pe-
' culiar in him on them all, that conquered
' the Minds, as well as it commanded the
' Attention of his Hearers; who felt all the
' while that they were learning fomewhat,
' and were never tired by him ; for he cut
' off both the Luxuriances of Stile, and the
' Length of Sermons ; and he concluded
' them with fome Thoughts of fuch Gra-
' vity and Ufe, that he generally difmiffed
                          ' his

' his Hearers with somewhat that stuck to
' them. He read his Sermons with so due
' a Pronunciation, in so sedate and solemn
' a manner, that they were not the feebler,
' but rather the perfecter, even by that
' way which often lessens the Grace, as
' much as it adds to the Exactness of such
' Discourses.

' He saw, with a deep Regret, the fatal
' Corruption of this Age, while the Hypo-
' crisies and Extravagancies of former
' Times, and the Liberties and Loosness
' of the present, disposed many to Atheism
' and Impiety. He therefore went far in-
' to this Matter: And as he had considered
' all the ancient and modern *Apologies* for
' the *Christian Religion*, with an Exactness
' that became the Importance of the Sub-
' ject, so he set the whole Strength of his
' Thoughts and Studies to withstand the
' Progress that this was making. In order
' to that he laboured particularly to bring
' every thing out of the clearest Princi-
' ples, and to make all People feel the Rea-
' sonableness of the Truths, as well as of
' the Precepts of the Christian Religion.
' When he saw that *Popery* was at the Root
' of this, and that the Design seemed to
' be laid, to make us first *Atheists*, that
' we might be the more easily made *Pa-*
' *pists*, and that many did not stick to own,
' that we could have no Certainty for the
' Chri-

' Chriftian Faith, unlefs we believed the
' *Infallibility of the Church.* This gave him
' a deep and juft Indignation: It was
' fuch a betraying of the Caufe of God,
' rather than not to gain their own, that
' in this the Foundation was laid of his
' great Zeal againft Popery. This drew
' his Studies for fome Years much that
' way: He looked on the whole Com-
' plex of Popery as fuch a Corruption of
' the whole Defign of Chriftianity, that he
' thought it was incumbent on him, to fet
' himfelf againft it; with the Zeal and
' Courage which became that Caufe, and
' was neceffary for thofe Times: He thought
' the Idolatry and Superftition of the
' Church of *Rome* did enervate true Piety
' and Morality ; and that their Cruelty
' was fuch a Contradiction to the Meek-
' nefs of Chrift, and to that Love and
' Charity which he made the Character
' and Diftinction of his Difciples and Fol-
' lowers, that he refolved to facrifice every
' thing, except a good Confcience, in a
' Caufe for which he had refolved, if it
' fhould come to Extremities, to become
' a Sacrifice to, himfelf.

' His Enemies foon faw how much he
' ftood in their Way, and were not want-
' ing in the Arts of Calumny, to difable
' him from oppofing them with that great
' Succefs which his Writings and Sermons
                                             ' had

' had on the Nation. His Life was too
' Pure in all the Parts of it, to give them a
' Pretence to attempt on that. So regu-
' lar a Piety, such an unblemished Probi-
' ty, and so extensive and tender a Chari-
' ty, together with his great and constant
' Labours, both in private and publick,
' set him above Reproach. That *Honour-*
' *able Society* * which treated him always
' with so particular a Respect, and so ge-
' nerous a Kindness; and this great City,
' not only the Neighbourhood of this Place,
' which was so long Happy in him, but the
' whole Extent of it, knew him too well,
' and esteemed him too much, for those
' his Enemies to adventure on the common
' Arts of defaming; subtle Methods were
' to be used, since his Virtue was too ex-
' emplary to be foiled in the ordinary
' way.
' His endeavouring to make out every
' Thing in Religion from clear and plain
' Principles, and with a Fulness of demon-
' strative Proof, was laid hold on to make
' him pass for one that could believe no-
' thing that lay beyond the Compass of
' Human Reason: And his tender Me-
' thod of treating with *Dissenters*, his En-
' deavours to extinguish that Fire, and to

---

* *Lincolns-Inn.*

' unite

' unite us among our felves, againſt thoſe
' who underſtood their own Intereſt well,
' and purſued it cloſely; inflaming our Dif-
' ferences, and engaging us into violent A-
' nimoſities, while they ſhifted Sides, and
' ſtill gained Ground, whether in the Me-
' thods of *Toleration*, or of a ſtrict Execu-
' tion of *Penal Laws*, as it might ſerve their
' Ends; thoſe calm and wiſe Deſigns of his,
' I ſay, were repreſented as a want of Zeal
' in the Cauſe of the Church, and an Incli-
' nation towards thoſe who departed from
' it. But how unhappily ſucceſsful ſoever
' they might be, in infuſing thoſe Jealou-
' ſies of him, into ſome warm and unwary
' Men, he ſtill went on in his own way:
' He would neither depart from his *Mode-*
' *ration*, nor take pains to cover himſelf
' from ſo falſe an Imputation. He thought
' the Openneſs of his Temper, the Courſe
' of his Life, his Sincerity, and the viſible
' Effects of his Labours, which had con-
' tributed ſo much to turn the greateſt part
' of this vaſt City to a hearty Love of the
' Church, and a firm adhering to the Com-
' munion of it, in which no Man was ever
' more eminently diſtinguiſh'd than he
' was: He thought, I ſay, that conſtant
' Zeal with which he had always ſerved
' ſuch as came to labour in this great City,
' and by which he had been ſo ſingularly
' uſeful to them; he thought the great

' Change

' Change that had been made in bringing
' Mens Minds off from many wild Opini-
' ons, to fober and fteady Principles, and
' that in fo prudent a manner, that Things
' were done without Men's perceiving it,
' or being either ftartled or fretted by the
' Peevifhnefs which is raifed and kept up
' by Contradiction or Difputing, in which,
' without derogating from other Mens La-
' bours, no Man had a larger Share than
' himfelf; upon all thefe Reafons, I fay,
' he thought that his Conduct needed no
' Apology, but that it was above it.

' After the Reftoration of the Church,
' Anger upon thofe Heads was both more
' in fafhion, and feemed more excufable:
' Men coming then out of the Injuftice and
' Violence by which they had been fo long
' ill ufed, and were fo much provoked; yet
' neither that, nor the Narrownefs of his
' Fortune, while he needed Supports, and
' faw what was the fhorteft Way to arrive
' at them, could make him change his
' Strain.

' His Life was not only free from Ble-
' mifhes, which is but a low fize of Com-
' mendation; it fhined in all the Parts of
' it. In his Domeftick Relations, in his
' Friendfhips, in the whole Commerce of
' Bufinefs, he was always a Pattern, eafie
' and humble, frank and open, tender-
' hearted and bountiful, kind and obliging,

' in

' in the greatest as well as the smallest Mat-
' ters : A decent but grave Chearfulness
' made his Conversation as lively and a-
' greeable, as it was useful and instruct-
' ing : He was ever in good Humour, al-
' ways the same, both accessible and affa-
' ble : He heard every thing patiently :
' Was neither apt to mistake nor to suspect :
' His own great Candor disposing him to
' put the best Constructions, and to judge
' the most favourably of all Persons and
' Things : He past over many Injuries,
' and was ever ready to forgive the great-
' est, and to do all good Offices even to
' those who had used him very ill. He
' was never imperious nor assuming : And
' tho' he had a superior Judgment to most
' Men, yet he never dictated to others :
' Few Men had observed Human Nature
' more carefully, could judge better, and
' make larger Allowances for the Frailties
' of Mankind than he did. He lived in
' a due neglect of his Person, and con-
' tempt of Pleasure, but never affected
' pompous Severities : He despised Wealth,
' but as it furnished him for Charity, in
' which he was both liberal and judicious.

' Thus his Course in the private Virtues
' and Capacities of a Christian was of a
' sublime pitch : His Temper had made
' him incapable of the Practices either of
' Craft or Violence.

K   ' In

' In his Function, he was a constant.
' Preacher, and diligent in all the other
' Parts of his Duty : For tho' he had no
' Care of Souls upon him, yet few that
' had, laboured so painfully as he did ; in
' Visiting the Sick, in Comforting the
' Afflicted, and in settling such as were
' either shaken in their Opinions, or
' troubled in Mind. He had a great Com-
' pass in Learning : What he knew, he had
' so perfectly digested, that he was truly
' the Master of it. But the Largeness of
' his Genius, and the Correctness of his
' Judgment, carried him much farther,
' than the leisure that he had enjoyed for
' Study, seemed to furnish him : For he
' could go a great way upon general Hints.
' Thus he lived, thus he run, and thus he
' *finished his Course.*
' He *kept the Faith.* If Fidelity is meant
' by this, no Man made Promises more
' unwillingly, but observed them more
' Religiously than he did. The sacred
' Vows of his Function were Conscienci-
' ously pursued by him ; he reckoned himself
' dedicated to the Service of God, and to
' the doing of Good. In this he lived,
' and seemed to live to no other end. But
' if by *keeping the Faith,* be to be under-
' stood the preserving and handing down
' the sacred Trust of the Christian Do-
' ctrine, this he maintained pure and un-
' defiled.

' defiled. Even in his younger Days,
' when he had a great Liveliness of
' Thought, and Fineness of Imagination,
' he avoided the disturbing the Peace of
' the Church with particular Opinions, or
' an angry Opposition about more indiffe-
' rent, or doubtful Matters: He lived in-
' deed in great Friendship with Men that
' differed from him: He thought the fu-
' rest Way to bring them off from their
' Mistakes, was by gaining upon their
' Hearts and Affections: And in an Age
' of such great Dissolution, as this is, he
' judged that the best Way to put a stop
' to growing Impiety, was first to establish
' the Principles of Natural Religion, and
' from that to advance to the Proof of the
' Christian Religion, and of the Scriptures:
' Which being once solidly done, would
' soon settle all other Things. Therefore
' he was in great doubt, whether the fu-
' rest Way to perswade the World, to the
' Belief of the sublime Truths that are
' contain'd in the Scriptures, concerning
' *God, the Father, the Son and the Holy*
' *Ghost*, and concerning the *Person of*
' *Christ*, was to enter much into the dif-
' cussing of those Mysteries: He feared
' that an indiscreet dwelling and descant-
' ing upon those things, might do more
' hurt than good: He thought the main-
' taining these Doctrines as they are propo-

' sed

' fed in the Scriptures, without entring too
' much into Explanations or Controverfies,
' would be the moſt effectual way to pre-
' ſerve the Reverence that was due to
' them, and to fix them in Mens Belief.
' But when he was defired by ſome, and
' provoked by others, and ſaw juſt Occa-
' ſions moving him to it, he aſſerted thoſe
' great Myſteries with that Strength and
' Clearneſs, that was his peculiar Talent.
' He thought the leſs Mens Conſciences
' were entangled, and the leſs the Com-
' munion of the Church was clogg'd with
' diſputable Opinions, or Practices, the
' World would be the Happier, Conſcien-
' ces the freer, and the Church the quieter.
' He made the Scriptures the meaſure of
' his Faith, and the chief Subject of all his
' Meditations.

' He indeed judged that the great Defign
' of Chriſtianity was the reforming Mens
' Natures, and governing their Actions,
' the reſtraining their Appetites and Paſſi-
' ons, the ſoftening their Tempers, and
' ſweetening their Humours, the compoſing
' their Affections, and the raiſing their
' Minds above the Intereſts and Follies
' of this preſent World, to the Hope and
' Purſuit of endleſs Bleſſedneſs: And he
' confidered the whole Chriſtian Doctrine
' as a Syſtem of Principles, all tending to
' this. He looked on Mens contending a-
　　　　　　　　　　　　　　　' bout

' bout leſſer Matters, or about Subtleties
' relating to thoſe that are greater, as one
' of the chief Practices of the Powers of
' Darkneſs, to defeat the true Ends *for*
' *which the Son of God came into the World,*
' and that they did lead Men into much
' dry and angry Work, who while they
' were hot in the making Parties, and ſet-
' tling Opinions, became ſo much the ſlacker
' in thoſe great Duties, which were chiefly
' deſigned by the Chriſtian Doctrine.

' I have now viewed him in this Light,
' in which St. *Paul* does here view himſelf,
' and have conſidered how much of that
' Character belonged to him : I have rea-
' ſon to believe that he went over theſe
' Things often in his own Thoughts, with
' the ſame proſpect that St. *Paul* had : For
' tho' he ſeem'd not to apprehend that
' Death was ſo near him, as it proved to
' be, yet he thought it was not far from
' him : He ſpoke often of it as that which
' he was longing for, and which he would
' welcome with Joy.

We ſee that this is but a ſummary View
of this Great Man, and ſuch a one as car-
ries with it all the Marks of Truth, Candor, and Sincerity. If we ſhould add the
Character which others, leſs ſuſpected by
ſome of partiality than the foregoing Author, gives, we ſhall find that they exceed

whac

what his Friend had said. Dean SHER-
LOCK speaking of the Great and Noble
Designs Queen *MARY* * had form'd to
promote true Religion, and the Service of
the Church of *England*, could not help upon this Occasion giving a just Encomium
upon the Arch-Bishop in the following
Manner. 'I have *(says he)* Reason to say this
' from those frequent Intimations I have
' had from our late admirable *Primate*,
' who had great Designs himself to serve
' the Christian Religion, and the Church
' of *England*, in its *truest Interests*; and had
' inspir'd their MAJESTIES, and particu-
' larly the QUEEN, who had more leisure
' for such Thoughts, with the same great
' and pious Designs; it may be no Church-
' man ever had, and I am sure, not more
' deservedly, a greater Interest in his
' PRINCE's Favour; and the great Use he
' made of it was to do publick Service to
' Religion, and whatever some Men might
' suspect, to the Church of *England*, tho'
' it may be not perfectly in their Way;
' and the greatest Fault, I knew he had,
' was, that some Envious and Ambitious
' Men could not bear his Greatness, which
' he himself never courted, nay, which
' he industriously avoided. Before this,

---

* *See, his Sermon preached at the* Temple *on the* Queen's
Death.

'all

' all *England* knew, and own'd his Worth;
' and had it been put to the *Poll*, there had
' been vaft odds on his Side, that he
' would have been voted into the See of
' *Canterbury*; for no Man had ever a clear-
' er and brighter Reafon, a truer Judg-
' ment, or more eafy and happy Expreffi-
' on, nor a more inflexible fearlefs Honefty:
' He was a true and hearty Friend where-
' ever he profefs'd to be fo; tho' he had
' many Enemies at laft, he took care to
' make none; he was obliging to all Men;
' and tho' he could not eafily part with a
' Friend, he could eafily forgive an Ene-
' my. But I cannot give you the Chara-
' &ter of this Great Man now; what I
' have already faid, I confefs, is an Ex-
' curfion, which I hope you will pardon,
' to the Paffion of an old Friend; and
' learn from Two great Examples, that
' neither the greateft Inocence, Virtue,
' or Merit, can defend either *Crown'd* or
' *Mitred* Heads from the Lafh of fpiteful
' and envenom'd Tongues.' Thus far
Dean SHERLOCK. Another Friend fays
of him, *When he was importun'd to ufe his*
Intereft with great Men for his Friends, upon
any Vacancies of Preferment in their Gift, he
would fometimes defire to be excufed from it,
telling them that he had often paid dear for fuch
Favours, fince he had been forced in return,
and upon their requeft, to give Livings to
K 4 ' others,

others, which were of double or treble Value to those he had obtain'd from them, and yet this could not be avoided; and therefore he intreated those who had Expectations from him, patiently to wait till Preferments fell, which were in his own Gift, and Disposal.

Not to add the many *Panegyricks* upon him from printed Books, I can't pass by one from a Manuscript *Diary* of a late learned and pious Divine, because there is a Particular in it which must arise from a personal Knowledge of Bishop TILLOT-SON. *He taught* (says he) *by his Sermons, more Ministers to Preach well, and more People to Live well, than any other Man since the Apostles Days ; he was the Ornament of the last Century, and the Glory of his Function; in the Pulpit another* CHRYSOSTOM, *and in the Episcopal Chair a Second* CRANMER. *He was so exceeding Charitable, that while in a private Station, he always laid aside Two Tenths of his Income for charitable Uses.*

Of his GRACE's Writings, one Volume in *Folio,* consisting of Fifty Two Sermons, and the *Rule* of *Faith,* were published in his Life Time, and corrected by his own Hand. Those which came Abroad after his Death from his *Chaplain* Dr. BARKER, make Two *Volumes* in *Folio,* the Value of which, if we may judge from the Price of the Copy, being Two Thousand Five Hundred Guineas, is not inferior to the for-

former. This, indeed, was the only Legacy he left to his Family, his extenfive Charity confuming his yearly Revenues as conftantly as they came to his Hands. If Charity be the Characteriftick of a true Difciple, furely he who exhaufted all he had in the nobleft manner, and trufted in Providence for the future Support of his own Family, deferves that Name more truly, than any in thefe late corrupted Ages can pretend to. But the *God* whom he ferved in the ftricteft of the Letter of the Commandment, fuffered not them to want, the *Royal Bounty* exerting it felf to his *Widow*, as I find in the two following Grants, taken from the Original Records in the Office of the Rolls in *Chancery-lane*, *viz.*

ANNO 7º GULIEL. *Tertio.*
' The KING (*May* 2.) granteth unto
' ELIZABETH TILLOTSON, Widow, and
' Relict of JOHN late Arch-Bifhop of *Canterbury*, an Annuity of 400*l.* during the
' Term of her natural Life.

ANNO 10º GULIEL. *Tertio.*
' The KING (*Auguft* 18th) granteth
' unto ELIZABETH TILLOTSON, Relict
' of Arch-Bifhop TILLOTSON, 200 *l. per*
' *Annum*, as an Addition to her Annuity
' of 400 *l. per Annum*, granted to her by
' Letters Patents dated *May* 2. 1695.

As

As to the Family of the Arch-Bishop, all that we can learn of them is, that his *Lady* was the *Daughter* of Dr. FRENCH, whose Widow *Bishop* WILKINS married. Of his Children we can say no more, than that he himself mentions the Loss of his only *Son* in his Letter to Mr. HUNT, and that he has a *Daughter* still living, married to JAMES CHADWICK, *Esq*; to whom Bishop WILLIAMS dedicates his Vindication of his GRACE's Sermons from the Charge of *Socinianism*. Thus much could we collect of this Great *Man*, which tho' but imperfect, the *Bishop* of *Salisbury*, who supplied us with some *Memoirs*, and promising us many more, dying while this Work was in hand; but if any one can give us any farther Notices of any Thing that relates to him, we shall hereafter insert them with all due Acknowledgment and Gratitude.

In the Church of St. *Lawrence Jewry*, on the left Side of the Communion Table, a very neat Marble Monument is erected to his Memory, with his Effigies in *Busto*, as here exactly delineated.

P. M
Reverendissimi & Sanctissimi Praesulis
IOANNIS TILLOTSON,
Archiepiscopi Cantuariensis,
Concionatoris olim hâc in Ecclesiâ
per annos XXX celeberrimi
Qui obijt X° Kal. Dec. MDCLXXXXIV
Ætatis suæ LXIIII
Hoc posuit Elizabetha
Conjux illius mœstissima

In the Year 1706, Mr. LUPTON, A. M. and Fellow of *Lincoln College* in *Oxford*, published a Sermon, in which he falls in a most violent Manner upon this great and good Man, on Account of his Sermon on the *Eternity of Hell Torments*. In this Invective the young Author (for I cannot think him very old, either by the Force of his Arguments, or the Candor of his Management of them) expresses a great deal of Warmth against the Bishop, and if hard Words, and malicious Insinuations, a Confidence of asserting, and an assuming Air throughout, are Proofs of a good Cause, and the better of the Argument, Mr. LUPTON has obtain'd the Victory over Arch-Bishop TILLOTSON; but if these are only the visible Effects of a vain Opinion of himself, we never had a Piece fuller of Vanity and Affectation.

This, and some other Efforts of this Nature, produc'd an excellent Vindication of the dead Prelate, by Mr. LE CLERC, which being added to this Life, it has saved me the Trouble of a particular Answer to this Piece. Yet I cannot wholly be silent on this Head, but shall throw in only two or three Reflections *en passant*.

First then, I can't help declaring, that from the Discourse I dare believe, that the Author, with all his Self Opinion, and
Assu-

Affurance, wou'd not have prefum'd to
publifh it, had not the great Man he attack'd been dead, and by Confequence
not able to defend himfelf. I muft farther obferve, that he does not pretend to
affert, that the *Eternity of Punifhments* is
deny'd by the Bifhop, but will not allow
that his Arguments are fufficient to prove
it, and therefore he fupplies better, as he
would have us believe.

I fhall give but a Specimen of his Con-
futation of the Bifhop's Argument, *That to
Punifh eternally Man for temporary Crimes,
can never be juftify'd by the common Reafon
that is brought in its Defence, viz.* That if
the Wicked fhould live always they wou'd
Sin on to *Eternity, for that it feems not agreeable to eternal Juftice to punifh Crimes that
never were committed.* But fays our Author,
*If the Sinner has provok'd God to that degree
as to make him with-hold his* faving Grace,
*then the Confequence is plain, that the Sinner
not being able to repent, or turn, without
that faving Grace, he muft inevitably Sin on
to Eternity, and is therefore juftly punifhed by*
Eternal Torments.

But can there be any Thing in Nature
more abfurd than this? to folve the Difficulty that lay againft the common Argument, that the Wicked wou'd Sin on eternally if they liv'd fo long; he wou'd fix a
greater Injuftice on God than the former

Ar-

Argument had done, for here he makes
God punish the Sinner for not repenting,
when he with-holds the only Means of his
being capable of doing so, *viz. saving
Grace.*

But this Place will not afford Room for
the prosecuting of this Point so far as it
may be carry'd; and to dwell on one, and
leave the rest untouch'd, might make him
and his Fautors think them unanswerable.
Besides, Mr. Le Clerc has done it more
largely, and more closely, and beyond a
Reply.

This Author's Arguments are indeed all
a mere begging of the Question, in taking
that for granted which wants chiefly to be
prov'd. If he had thought the Arch-Bishop had weaken'd, or gone against any
Doctrine of the Scripture, he ought first
to have fixt his Sense of the Texts on which
he built this Doctrine. For Example, he
ought particularly to have shown that the
Scripture was to be taken litterally here,
tho' not in other Places, and given irre-
fragable Arguments to prove why it should
be so. He should have shown, that *for ever*,
Everlasting, &c. in the Scripture Sense,
were always understood as we do now, or
as he does, of something that never can or
will have an End. *One Generation cometh,
and another goeth, but the Earth endures* FOR
EVER, is a Text in Scripture, and yet I
be-

believe this Gentleman will not contend
that there is to be no End of the *Earth*,
and yet tell us he believes the Bible. It being notorious, that as the Scripture often
by *all the Earth* only means the Land of *Ju-
dah*, or of *Israel*; so those Terms of, *for e-
ver, always,* and *everlasting*, are frequently
made use of to express a long Duration of
Time which yet will have an End.

He should therefore have clear'd this
Point in the first Place, and evidently have
shown why those Words shou'd bear in this
Case a different Sense.

I shall say no more to this Author,
but leave the Reader to the following Discourse of Mr. LE CLERC, which before
he peruses, I think it proper to insert a
Letter relating to this Matter, which I
receiv'd from the Reverend Mr. PEARSE,
Vice-Principal of *Edmund-Hall* in *Oxford*.

SIR,

'IT is a common Practice with Persons
   ' who have not Abilities sufficient to
' perform any Work by which they may be-
' come known to the World, to endeavour
' at a Name and Character, by raking into
' the Ashes, and blackening the Reputati-
' on of Men of real Worth, Piety, and
' Learning. The eminent Prelate, whose
' Life you are about to publish, has been
                              ' aspersed,

' afperfed, and fuffered fufficiently in this
' kind. One has thought fit to call him a
' *Grave Atheift* : Another, a *Thorough-pac'd*
' *Phanatic* : And a Third, a *Trifler*, and a
' Denyer of Eternal Punifhments in ano-
' ther World. The firft of thefe, 'tis well
' known, did it out of *Zeal*, *Heat*, and
' *Party* : The fecond, by miftaking his
' *Piety* and *Moderation* for *Phanaticifm* !
' And the third, was acted by an *ambitious*
' *Ignorance*. Dr. HICKES's efpecial Friend,
' in his Life of Bifhop BULL, has recom-
' mended a Reverend Gentleman as a Pat-
' tern to the *young Preachers who are now*
' *growing up*, for no other Reafon that is
' known to the World, but for a weak
' Endeavour to leffen the Name of Arch-
' Bifhop TILLOTSON. Had he ferioufly
' and impartially confider'd Matters, he
' would have fet the Bifhop's Sermons as a
' Pattern, whofe Genius, Method, Senfe,
' and Language, are as much fuperior to
' any of his Adverfaries, as his Station was
' in the Church. Bifhop TILLOTSON does
' indeed in his Sermon of *Hell Torments*,
' give the Objections their full force, but
' then in the Conclufion, he declares his
' Opinion of their *eternal Duration*, in the
' moft pathetical manner imaginable. It
' has been a fault in feveral learned Men,
' not to be as large and clear in their An-
' fwers as they were in their Objections.

' But

' But then no Person of Honesty, Sense,
' or Religion, will infer from thence that
' they were Heterodox, and held the
' wrong Side of the Question. A Reve-
' rend Divine in his *Conference with a Deift*,
' has for Instance, stated the Arguments
' for Deism much stronger than his An-
' swers to them, and yet no Man ever
' thought him inclinable to Theism, but
' Honest and Orthodox. I mention this
' of Bishop TILLOTSON's Sermon, because
' I have been inform'd, That I was in
' some measure the Occasion of Dr. LUP-
' TON's printing his Discourse in answer to
' it. Had not a Discourse of Bishop BULL's
' on that Subject been lost, perhaps the
' World would have seen all that could
' have been said for, and against, the Que-
' stion, fairly stated.

' But that which makes me write to you
' at present, chiefly is, to communicate
' to you, a Memorandum found in the
' Study of the Reverend Mr. CREECH,
' which a Person gave me some Years since,
' when his Books were Sold by Auction
' here in *Oxford*. It reflects exceedingly
' on the Bishop, and deserves to be taken
' Notice of by the Publisher of his Life.
' 'Tis as follows, *viz.*

' Memorandum, *That whatever Steps
' were taken, and all that was done, for the
' abolishing of Episcopacy, and subversion of*
' the

' the Church of Scotland, *was done by the*
' *Contrivance, Advice, and Approbation of*
' Dr. TILLOTSON. And then he adds,
' *This I had from* Johnson, *who was certain*
' *of, and knew the whole Matter, when I was*
' *down in the North* *.

' This, Sir, is what I thought fit to
' communicate to you, upon reading your
' Advertisement in the News Papers. I
' am, Sir,

Your obedient,

Oxford, *Edmund Hall,*   *humble Servant,*
Jan. 11th. 1715.

ROB. PEARSE.

---

* *See* Page 6. *for an Answer to this* Memorandum.

A
DEFENCE
OF

Archbifhop TILLOTSON,

AND HIS

WRITINGS.

By Monfieur Le Clerc.

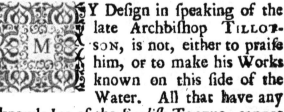

MY Defign in fpeaking of the late Archbifhop Tillot-son, is not, either to praife him, or to make his Works known on this fide of the Water. All that have any knowledge of the Englifh Tongue, cannot but be acquainted with them. Befides, the Merit of this great Man is far above

B   my

my Praifes; and to write the Elogium of a Perfon to whom every Body gives a good Character, is not the way to afford my Readers much Satisfaction. Should I go about to do it, I muft defcribe a Man excellent for a clear Head, great Penetration, exquifite Reafoning, profound Knowledge of true Divinity, and folid Piety, for a peculiar Plainnefs and Elegance of Stile without any Affectation; and in fhort, endow'd with all that could be wifh'd in one of that Order. To crown his good Qualities, I ought to add, that they were too eminent not to draw on him Envy and Calumny; which very feldom attack the common People, or Men of ordinary Qualifications. I ought alfo to put the World in mind that he has been accus'd of *Socinianifm*; which has commonly been laid to the Charge of fuch as have reafon'd better than the Vulgar, and preferr'd the Scripture Phrafe to the School-Terms. Thefe Calumnies, inftead of tarnifhing the Reputation of fuch Men as Archbifhop TILLOTSON, are Foils to fet it off, and only heighten it, like Shades in a Picture; efpecially when repell'd after his manner. I fhall not examine thofe Accufations, but only tell the World, that after his Death there was found a bundle of bitter Libels that had been vented againft him, on which he had wrote with his own Hand,

I

I FORGIVE THE AUTHORS OF THESE BOOKS, AND PRAY GOD THAT HE MAY ALSO FORGIVE THEM. All thofe Calumnies did him little hurt during his Life, for he attain'd to the higheft Dignities of the Church of *England*; and fince his Death they are all fallen to the Ground.

Every Body knows that Sermons are commonly fill'd with a flafhy Rhetoric, which takes much better from the Pulpit than the Prefs; but Archbifhop TILLOTSON's are for the moft part exact Diſſertations, which will bear being examin'd by the ftricteft Reafoners. Tho' fuch of them as he publifh'd during his Life, with his Treatife of *The Rule of Faith*, are the exacteft, and the moft labour'd, yet thofe that have been publifh'd fince his Death, have been extremely lik'd, and defervedly efteemed.

As few of his Sermons have been feen here, I fhall give an Extract of the Thirty Fifth, which treats of the *Eternity of Hell Torments*; this fome of my Friends have defir'd to fee, on Account of a Quotation I formerly made out of it.

I fhall alfo add a few Remarks, and draw fome Confequences which appear proper for the Defence of the *Chriftian Religion*, againft thofe that reject it upon account of its teaching the Eternity of the Pains of the next Life.

‘ This

' This eternal State of Rewards and
' Punifhments in another World (fays
' Archbifhop TILLOTSON) our *Bleffed Sa-*
' *viour* hath clearly revealed to us. And
' as to one part of it, *viz.* That good
' Men fhall be eternally happy in another
' World, every one gladly admits it : But
' many are loth that the other part fhould
' be true, concerning the eternal Punifh-
' ment of wicked Men. And therefore
' they pretend that it is contrary to the Ju-
' ftice of God to punifh temporary Crimes
' with eternal Torments : Becaufe Juftice
' always obferves a proportion between
' Offences and Punifhments ; but between
' temporary Sins and eternal Punifhments
' there is no proportion. And as this
' feems hard to be reconciled with Juftice,
' fo much more with that excefs of Good-
' nefs which we fuppofe to be in God.

' And therefore they fay, that though
' God feems to have declared that impeni-
' tent Sinners fhall be everlaftingly pu-
' nifh'd, yet thefe Declarations of Scrip-
' ture are fo to be mollified and underftood,
' as that we may be able to reconcile them
' with the effential Perfections of the Di-
' vine Nature.

' This is the full Force and Strength of
' the Objection. And my Work at this
' Time fhall be to clear, if I can, this dif-
' ficult Point. And that for thefe two
                                    ' Rea-

' Reasons. *First,* For the Vindication of
' the Divine Justice and Goodness : *That*
' *God may be justified in his Sayings, and ap-*
' *pear Righteous when he judgeth,* And Se-
' *condly,* Because the Belief of the Threat-
' nings of God in their utmost extent is of
' so great a moment to a good Life, and
' so great a discouragement to Sin ; for
' the Sting of Sin is the Terror of eternal
' Punishment; and if Men were once set
' free from the fear and belief of this, the
' most powerful restraint from Sin would
' be taken away.

' So that in answer to that Objection, I
' shall endeavour to prove these two
' Things.

' *First,* That the eternal Punishment of
' wicked Men in another World is plainly
' threatned in Scripture.

' *Secondly,* That this is not inconsistent
' either with the Justice or the Goodness of
' God.

' *First,* That the eternal Punishment of
' wicked Men in another World, is plain-
' ly threatned in Scripture, namely, in
' these following *Texts,* Mat. 18. 18. *It is*
' *better for thee to enter into Life halt and*
' *maimed, than having two hands or two*
' *feet to be cast into everlasting Fire.* And
' *Mat.* 25. 41. *Depart ye cursed into ever-*
' *lasting Fire, prepared for the Devil and his*
' *Angels.* And here in the *Text, these,*

' that

' that is, *the wicked shall go away into ever-*
' *lasting Punishment.* And *Mark* 9. it is
' there three several Times with great
' vehemency repeated by our *Saviour,*
' *where their worm dieth not, and the fire is*
' *not quenched.* And 2 *Theff.* 1. 9. speak-
' ing of *them that know not God, and obey*
' *not the Gospel of his Son.* It is said of
' them, *who shall be punished with everlasting*
' *destruction.*

' I know very well that great Endea-
' vour hath been used to avoid the Force of
' these *Texts,* by shewing that the Words,
' for *ever* and *everlasting,* are frequently
' us'd in Scripture in a more limitted Sense,
' only for a long duration and continuance.
' Thus, for *ever,* doth very often in the
' *Old Testament* only signifie for a long time,
' and till the end of the *Jewish* Dispensati-
' on. And in the *Epistle* of St. *Jude, verse*
' *7th.* The Cities of *Sodom* and *Gomorrah*
' are said to be *set forth for an Example,*
' *suffering the vengeance of eternal Fire,* that
' is, of a Fire that was not extinguished till
' those Cities were utterly consumed.

There is no *Hebrew* Word which, properly speaking, signifies *Eternity,* or
a Time without end. עולם *Holam* means only
a Time, whose *beginning* or *end* is not
known; according to the meaning of its
Root, which signifies *to hide.* Thus it is
taken in a stricter, or less strict Sense, according

cording to what is treated of. When
God, or his Attributes are meant, this
Word is underſtood in its greateſt Extent;
that is, it means a true *Eternity*. But when
it is applied to Things which have a *beginning* and an *end*, it is then alſo taken in as limited a Senſe as the Thing requires. Thus
when God ſays concerning the *Jewiſh* Laws
that they muſt be obſerv'd, לעלם *leholam*,
for ever, we are to underſtand as long
a ſpace of Time as God ſhould think fit,
a ſpace whoſe end was unknown to the
Jews before the coming of the *Meſſiah*.
All general Laws, and ſuch as do not regard particular Occaſions and Circumſtan-
ces, are made for *ever*; whether it be expreſs'd in thoſe Laws or not; which yet
is not to be underſtood in ſuch manner, as
if the Sovereign Power could no way change
it. The *for ever* is conſtantly underſtood,
till the Sovereign thinks fit to change that
Law. So Archbiſhop TILLOTSON makes
it no difficulty.

' I ſhall readily grant, *ſays he*, that the
' Words, for *ever* and *everlaſting*, do not
' always in Scripture ſignifie an endleſs du-
' ration; and that this is ſufficiently pro-
' ved by the Inſtances alledg'd to this pur-
' poſe. But then, *Secondly*, It cannot be
' denied on the other hand, that theſe
' Words are often in Scripture uſed in a
' larger Senſe, and ſo as neceſſarily to ſig-

'nify

' nify an interminable and endlefs Durati-
' on. As where Eternity is attributed to
' God, and he is faid to *live ever and ever*:
' And where eternal Happinefs in another
' World is promifed to good Men, and
' that *they fhall be for ever with the Lord.*
' Now the very fame Words and Expreffi-
' ons are us'd concerning the Punifhment
' of wicked Men in another Life, and there
' is great reafon why we fhould under-
' ftand them in the fame extent: Both,
' becaufe if God had intended to have told
' us that the Punifhment of wicked Men
' fhall have no end, the Languages where-
' in the Scriptures are written do hardly
' afford fuller and more certain Words,
' than thofe that are ufed in this cafe,
' whereby to exprefs to us a duration
' without end: And likewife, which is al-
' moft a peremptory decifion of the thing,
' becaufe the duration of the punifhment
' of wicked Men is in the very fame Sen-
' tence exprefs'd by the very fame word
' which is us'd for the duration of the Hap-
' pinefs of the Righteous: As is evident
' from the *Text, Thefe,* fpeaking of the
' wicked, *fhall go away,* εἰς κόλασιν αἰώνιον, *in-*
' *to eternal Punifhment,* but the righteous
' εἰς ζωὴν αἰώνιον, *into Life eternal.* I pro-
' ceed to the
 ' *Second* Thing I propos'd; namely, to
' fhew that this is not inconfiftent either
       ' with

' with the Juftice or the Goodnefs of God.
' For in this the force of the Objection lies.
' And it hath been attempted to be anfwer-
' ed feveral ways, none of which feems to
' me to give clear and full fatisfaction to it.

' *Firft*, It is faid by fome, that becaufe
' Sin is infinite in refpect of the Object a-
' gainft whom it is committed, which is
' God, therefore it deferves an infinite Pu-
' nifhment.

' But this I doubt will upon examinati-
' on be found to have more of fubtlety than
' of folidity in it. 'Tis true indeed, that
' the dignity of the Perfon againft whom
' any offence is committed is a great ag-
' gravation of the fault. For which rea-
' fon all offences againft God are certainly
' the greateft of all other: But that Crimes
' fhould hereby be heighten'd to an infinite
' degree can by no means be admitted;
' and that for this plain Reafon; becaufe
' then the evil and demerit of all Sins muft
' neceffarily be equal; for the demerit of
' no Sin can be more than infinite: And if
' the demerit of all Sins be equal, there can
' then be no reafon for the degrees of Pu-
' nifhment in another World: But to de-
' ny that there are degrees of Punifhment
' there, is not only contrary to Reafon, but to
' our *Saviour*'s exprefs affertion, that fome
' fhall be *beaten with many Stripes*, and fome
' with fewer, and that it fhall be *more to-*
' *lerable*

' lerable for some in the Day of Judgment
' than for others. Besides, that by the
' same Reason that the least Sin that is
' committed against God may be said to
' be infinite because of its Object, the least
' Punishment that is inflicted by God
' may be said to be infinite because of its
' Author; and then all Punishments from
' God as well as all Sins against him would
' be equal; which is palpably absurd. So
' that this answer is by no means suffici-
' ent to break the force of this Objection.

Besides, it may be obser" d, that the
Person against whom a Fault is committed, makes it to be greater, when it is directly against that Person, and not when
it regards him only indirectly. All the
Crimes that are committed in a Kingdom
are oppos'd to the Will of the Prince; yet
all are not Crimes of High-Treason, neither are they punish'd so severely. Crimes
of High-Treason are such as are committed with a Design to hurt the Person or
Authority of the Prince; and not all those
that are committed against the Laws of the
State. Thus in respect of God, Atheism
and all its Consequences are more directly
committed against God, and are much
greater Sins, than those which are Breaches of other Divine Laws. Besides, as to
the Aggravation of a Sin, we must have
regard to the Circumstances; as for Example,

ample, to the Degree of Knowledge of
them that fin, the Malice of their Behaviour, the ill Confequences of their Actions,
and other fuch Things. Thefe Circumftances do much more aggravate the Sin,
than the Object, againft which it was committed. Juftice requires the Weaknefs of
the Sinners to be confider'd, as well as the
Perfon againft whom the Sin is committed.

' It is faid by others, *continues Archbifhop*
' TILLOTSON, that if wicked Men lived
' for ever in this World, they would fin for
' ever, and therefore they deferve to be
' punifh'd for ever. But this hath neither
' Truth nor Reafon enough in it to give
' fatisfaction. For who can certainly tell
' that if a Man lived never fo long he
' would never repent and grow better?

' Befides that, the Juftice of God doth
' only punifh the Sins which Men have
' committed in this Life, and not thofe
' which they might poffibly have commit-
' ted if they had lived longer.

' *Thirdly*, It is faid in the laft Place, that
' God doth fet before Men everlafting
' Happinefs and Mifery, and the Sinner
' hath his choice. Here are two Things
' faid which bid fairly towards an anfwer.

' *Firft*, That the Reward which God
' promifeth to our Obedience is equal to
' the Punifhment which he threatens to
' our Difobedience ; but yet this I doubt
' will

' will not reach the Bufinefs; becaufe,
' though it be not contrary to Juftice to
' exceed in Rewards, that being matter
' of meer Favour; yet it may be fo to ex-
' ceed in Punifhments.

'*Secondly*, It is farther faid, that the
' Sinner in this Cafe hath nothing to com-
' plain of, fince he hath his own Choice.
' This I confefs is enough to filence the Sin-
' ner, and to make him to acknowledge
' that his Deftruction is of himfelf; but
' yet after all that, it does not feem fo
' clearly to fatisfy the Objection from the
' difproportion between the Fault and the
' Punifhment.

' And therefore I fhall endeavour to
' clear, if it may be, this matter yet a lit-
' tle farther by thefe following Confide-
' rations.

'*Firft*, Let it be confider'd, that the
' meafure of Penalties with refpect to
' Crimes, is not only, nor always to be ta-
' ken from the quality and degree of the
' offence, much lefs from the duration and
' continuance of it, but from the ends and
' reafons of Government; which requires
' fuch Penalties as may, if it be poffible,
' fecure the obfervation of the Law, and
' deter Men from the breach of it. And
' the reafon of this is evident, becaufe if
' it were once declar'd that no Man fhould
' fuffer longer for any Crime than accord-
'ing

' ing to the proportion of the Time in
' which it was committed, the Confe-
' quence of this would be, that Sinners
' would be better Husbands of their Time,
' and Sin fo much the fafter, that they
' might have the greater Bargain of it,
' and might fatisfy for their fins by a fhor-
' ter Punifhment.

' And it would be unreafonable likewife
' upon another Account ; becaufe fome of
' the greateft Sins may perhaps be commit-
' ted in the fhorteft time ; for Inftance,
' *Murder* ; the act whereof may be over
' in a moment, but the Effects of it are per-
' petual. For he that kills a Man once
' kills him for ever. The Act of Murder
' may be committed in a trice, but the
' Injury is endlefs and irreparable. So
' that this Objection of temporary Crimes
' being punifh'd with fo much longer Suf-
' ferings, is plainly of no force.

' Befides that, whoever confiders how
' ineffectual the threatning even of eternal
' Torments is to the greateft part of Sin-
' ners, will foon be fatisfy'd that a lefs Pe-
' nalty than that of eternal Sufferings,
' would to the far greateft part of Mankind
' have been in all probability of little or no
' force. And therefore, if any Thing more
' terrible than eternal Vengeance could
' have been threatned to the workers of
' Iniquity, it had not been unreafonable,

' becaufe

' becaufe it would all have been little e-
' nough to deter Men effectually from Sin.

' So that what Proportion Crimes and Pe-
' nalties ought to bear to each other, is
' not fo properly a confideration of Juftice,
' as of Wifdom and Prudence in the Law-
' giver.

' And the Reafon of this feems very
' plain, becaufe the meafure of Penalties
' is not taken from any ftrict Proportion
' betwixt Crimes and Punifhments, but
' from one great end and defign of Go-
' vernment, which is to fecure the obfer-
' vation of wholfome and neceffary Laws ;
' and confequently whatever Penalties are
' proper and neceffary to this end are not
' unjuft.

' And this Confideration I defire may be
' more efpecially obferved, becaufe it
' ftrikes at the very Foundation of the Ob-
' jection. For if the appointing and ap-
' portioning of Penalties to Crimes be not
' fo properly a confideration of Juftice,
' but rather of Prudence in the Lawgiver ;
' then whatever the difproportion may be
' between temporary Sins and eternal Suf-
' ferings, Juftice cannot be faid to be con-
' cern'd in it.

' Juftice indeed is concern'd, that the
' Righteous and the Wicked fhould not be
' treated alike ; and farther yet, that great-
' er Sins fhould have a heavier Punifhment,
' and

' and that *mighty Sinners should be mightily*
' *tormented*; but all this may be confider'd
' and adjufted in the degree and the intenf-
' nefs of the Suffering, without making a-
' ny difference in the duration of it.

' The cafe then in fhort ftands thus.
' Whenever we break the Laws of God,
' we fall into his Hands, and lye at his
' Mercy; and he may without injuftice
' inflict what Punifhment upon us he plea-
' feth: And confequently, to fecure his
' Law from violation, he may before hand
' threaten what Penalties he thinks fit,
' and neceffary to deter Men from the
' Tranfgreffion of it. And this is not efteem-
' ed unjuft among Men, to punifh Crimes
' that are committed in an inftant, with
' the perpetual lofs of Eftate, or Liberty,
' or Life.

For the right underftanding of this,
we muft know that the Pains fettled by the
Laws, are only appointed for one, or fome
one of thefe four Ends. The Firft, is to
repair the Injury, as when a Man is condemned to repair the wrong that he has
done to another. The Second, is to correct thofe that have committed a Fault,
whether they be punifh'd in their Goods or
Perfons; to the intent that People may
obferve the Laws and be honeft Men. The
Third, is to prevent Evil, by making an
Example of fome, to hinder others from
com-

committing the Diforders for which Punifhments are inflicted, and which would otherwife be prejudicial to Society. The Fourth, is to fatisfy offended Juftice, by impofing Pains proportional to the Crimes. Several Things may be found upon this Subject in GROTIUS, *de jure Belli & Pacis*, B. 2. Chap. 20. *And* PUFFENDORF *de jure Naturæ & Gentium*, B. 8. Chap 3.

The Pains of another Life are neither appointed for repairing an Injury, or making the Sinner to amend, nor for preventing Evil, at leaft at the Time that they are inflicted, as all the World now believes. But it is only of thofe Pains of which fome pretend to affirm that there is not an equal Proportion obferv'd between the Crime and its Punifhment. The Injury is greater or lefs, according to the Circumftances, and the Reparation varies alfo according to them, as may be learn'd in the forenam'd Authors; fo that fometimes, not upon account of the prefent Wrong, but upon account of the Confequences a Reparation is exacted, which is much greater than the Damage done. Oftentimes alfo to reform a People, or prevent an Evil, much more fevere Pains are inflicted than would otherwife be, if the People were not addicted to certain Vices, and if nothing was to be fear'd for the future.

ture. This is the Reason of the want
of Proportion, which sometimes appears
to be between the Punishments which
the Sovereigns inflict, and the Faults
which have been committed. But if we
throughly examine the Reasons why the
Sovereign does thus, supposing him just,
we shall not find such a Disproportion as
at first appears to be; because we shall
easily conceive, that the Circumstances in
which a State happens to be, do very
much diminish, or aggravate the Faults;
which are not so much consider'd in themselves, as in respect to the harm which
they may do to the State, if they are not
severely punish'd. That we may rightly
understand what Proportion there is between the Fault and the Punishment, we
must, together with the Fault, weigh all
the Evil which it wou'd cause at certain
Conjunctures, if it was not severely punish'd; for this is what the Sovereign con-
siders when he is govern'd by Wisdom, and
willing to observe Justice. Thus in this,
as well as in every Thing else, he must
observe the Rules of Justice, and of Proportion between the Faults and the Punishments. If the Sovereign, for the Reparation of a Damage, small in it self, and
which cou'd have no ill Consequences,
shou'd impose a Punishment altogether

C   difdisproportionable, he might very deservedly be said to be unjust.

Therefore I don't know, whether the Answer that Archbishop TILLOTSON gives here is altogether satisfactory. Nevertheless it may be said, that if God's Threats be consider'd in themselves, and before the Execution of them be seen (and that is the manner in which we consider them whilst we live) they may serve to repair the Wrong that is done to another, to better those that are frighted with them, and to prevent a great many Evils. If we consider them as being yet but Threats, and before their Execution, no Man can complain of them. Tho' they shou'd menace Pains much greater than one wou'd think cou'd be deserv'd by the Sins of so blind and frail a Creature as Man, and whose Consequences do not extend beyond this Earth or this Life; yet God cou'd not be said to be unjust, neither cou'd the Holy Scripture give us an ill Notion of his Justice; because we know that Threats are not executed with the utmost Rigour, and that more Severity is express'd than design'd, to fright those whom we love and wou'd keep in their Duty. The Case being thus, it may be said to quiet the Mind of those who are startled at the Eternity of the Punishments, that no one on Earth can

com

complain of the Divine Juſtice, in reſpeCt
to the Pains of the next Life; becauſe no
one yet knows what will be their Execution at the Day of Judgment, nor how the
Souls of wicked Men are treated now
when they die. Beſides, God has in this
Life given us ſo many Proofs of his Kindneſs, both in the Works of his general Providence, and in the Revelation of the Goſpel, that he very well deſerves that we
ſhou'd rely upon him in reſpeCt of the next
Life, and be perſwaded that he will do
nothing that is contrary to the ſtriCteſt Juſtice. If his Threats contain exceſſive Pains,
he has it always in his Power to moderate
them, as Equity ſhall require; and we
muſt not doubt but that he will do it, if
his Sovereign PerfeCtion engages him to it.
For my Part, I am perſwaded, that the
Clouds which darken our ſight being then
diſpers'd, the Wicked and the Good will
have equal Reaſon to acknowledge his
Juſtice on the one Hand; and on the other,
how much thoſe have been in the wrong
who have expos'd themſelves to the EffeCts
of it. Then let ſuch as find fault with the
Goſpel Revelation, becauſe it ſpeaks of
eternal Puniſhments, own themſelves in
the wrong, and forbear complaining till
they have ſeen the Execution of thoſe Puniſhments. Let them in the mean Time
entertain a favourable Opinion of the Di-

vine

vine Bounty and Juftice; judging of the
future by what is already pafs'd. Nothing unjuft is requir'd of them, and the
Advice which is given of them, cannot
but be very much for their Advantage.
It can be no prejudice to them, to have had
an high Opinion of God's Attributes, and
they hazard all in beginning, even in this
Life, to blafpheme againft their Maker, in
cenfuring his Revelation. Muft they for
the fatisfaction of an unreafonable Paffion
expofe themfelves to the moft fevere Effects
of the Divine Juftice, if there be a Divine
Juftice, as we have fuch Reafons to believe as they can by no means overthrow :
They are at leaft forc'd to confefs, that no
body can demonftrate the contrary ; and
in fuch a doubt, a Man muft be mad to
inveigh againft what he will find but too
true.

Laftly, I take no notice of the Fourth
End of Punifhments, inflicted, according
to fome, only to fatisfy offended Juftice ;
tho' it is ufual to refer to Punifhments of
that fort, thofe of the next Life ; becaufe
Archbifhop TILLOTSON takes no notice of
them in what he has juft faid; and what he
fays afterwards will anfwer all the Objections that can be rais'd on this Occafion,
concerning the Difproportion of the Faults
and the Punifhments.

' Secondly,

' Secondly, *says he,* This will yet appear
' more reasonable when we consider, that
' after all, he that threatens hath still the
' Power of Execution in his own Hands.
' For there is this remarkable difference
' between Promises and Threatnings; that
' he who promiseth passeth over a Right
' to another, and thereby stands obliged
' to him in Justice and Faithfulness to make
' good his Promise; and if he do not,
' the Party to whom the Promise is made,
' is not only disappointed, but injuriously
' dealt withal: But in Threatnings it is
' quite otherwise. He that threatens
' keeps the Right of punishing in his own
' Hand, and is not obliged to execute what
' he hath threatned, any further than the
' Reasons and Ends of Government do re-
' quire: And he may without any injury
' to the Party threatned, remit and abate
' as much as he pleaseth of the Punishment
' that he hath threatned; and because in
' so doing he is not worse but better than
' his Word, no Body can find fault, or
' complain of any wrong or injustice there-
' by done to him.
' Nor is this any Impeachment of God's
' Truth and Faithfulness, any more than
' it is esteem'd among Men a piece of
' Falshood not to do what they have
' threatned. God did absolutely threaten
' the Destruction of the City of *Niniveh,*

C 3 ' and

' and his peevish *Prophet* did understand
' the Threatning to be absolute, and was
' very angry with God for employing him
' in a Message that was not made good.
' But God understood his own Right, and
' did what he pleas'd notwithstanding the
' Threatning he had denounc'd; and for
' all *Jonah* was so touch'd in Honour, that
' he had rather have died himself than that
' *Niniveh* should not have been destroy'd,
' only to have verify'd his Message.

' I know it is said in this Case, that
' God hath confirm'd these Threatnings
' by an Oath, which is a certain sign of the
' immutability of his Counsel; and there-
' fore his Truth is concern'd in the strict
' and rigorous Execution of them. The
' Land of *Canaan* was a Type of Heaven,
' and the *Israelites* who rebell'd in the
' Wilderness were also a Type of impeni-
' tent Sinners under the Gospel; and con-
' sequently the Oath of God concerning
' the rebellious *Israelites,* when he *sware
' in his Wrath that they should not enter into
' his Rest,* that is, into the Land of *Ca-
' naan,* doth equally oblige him to execute
' his Threatning upon all impenitent Sin-
' ners under the Gospel, that *they shall ne-
' ver enter into the Kingdom of God.* And
' this is very truly reason'd, so far as the
' Threatning extends; which, if we at-
' tend to the plain Words of it, beyond
' which

' which Threatnings are never to be
' stretch'd, doth not seem to reach any
' further than to the exclusion of impe-
' nitent Sinners out of Heaven, and their
' falling finally short of the Rest and Hap-
' piness of the Righteous: Which how-
' ever, directly overthrows the Opinion
' ascrib'd to *Origen*, that the Devils and
' wicked Men shall all be saved at last;
' God having *sworn in his Wrath that they*
' *shall never enter into his Rest.*

Nevertheless, it is certain that whatever agrees with the Type does not necessarily agree with the Antitype; and that
this typical Divinity contains rather Ap-
plications of Passages to a Subject different
from that which they directly treat of,
than demonstrative Proofs. This is the
reason why School-men say that nothing
can be concluded from Symbols. *Theologia*
Symbolica non est Argumentativa. Except
the Scripture teaches us that God had regard to such and such Things, when he
expresses himself after such a particular
manner, we cannot speak of Types with
any certainty.

' But then, as to the eternal Misery and
' Punishment threatned to wicked Men in
' the other World, though it be not neces-
' sarily comprehended in this Oath, that
' they *shall not enter into his Rest*; yet we

C 4   ' are

' are to consider, that both the tenor of
' the *Sentence* which our blessed *Saviour*
' hath assur'd us will be pass'd upon them
' at the Judgment of the great Day, *De-*
' *part ye cursed into everlasting Fire*; and
' likewise this Declaration in the Text,
' that *the Wicked shall go away into everlasting*
' *Punishment*; though they do not restrain
' God from doing what he pleases, yet
' they cut off from the Sinner all reasona-
' ble hopes of the relaxation or mitigation
' of them. For since the great Judge of
' the World hath made so plain and ex-
' press a Declaration, and will certainly
' pass such a Sentence, it would be the
' greatest folly and madness in the World
' for the Sinner to entertain any hope of
' escaping it, and to venture his Soul upon
' that hope.

' I know but one Thing more, common-
' ly said upon this Argument, that seems
' material. And that is this, that the
' Words *Death* and *Destruction*, and *Pe-*
' *rishing*, whereby the Punishment of wic-
' ked Men in the other World is most fre-
' quently express'd in *Scripture*, do most
' properly import *Annihilation*, and an ut-
' ter end of Being, and therefore may rea-
' sonably be so understood in the matter of
' which we are now speaking.

' To

' To this I anſwer, That theſe Words,
' and thoſe which anſwer them in other
' Languages, are often, both in *Scripture*,
' and other *Authors*, uſed to ſignifie a
' ſtate of great Miſery and Suffering, with-
' out the utter extinction of the miſerable.
' Thus God is often in *Scripture* ſaid to
' bring *deſtruction* upon a Nation when he
' ſends great Judgments upon them,
' though they do not exterminate and
' make an utter end of them.

' And nothing is more common in moſt
' Languages, than by *periſhing* to expreſs
' a Perſon's being undone and made very
' miſerable. As in that known Paſſage
' in *Tiberius*'s Letter to the *Roman* Senate.
' * *Let all the Gods and Goddeſſes*, ſaith he,
' *deſtroy me worſe than at this very Time I*
' *feel my ſelf to periſh*, &c. in which ſaying,
' the Words *deſtroy* and *periſh*, are both of
' them us'd to expreſs the miſerable An-
' guiſh and Torment which at that Time
' he felt in his Mind, as *Tacitus* tells us at
' large.

' And as for the word Death; a State
' of Miſery, which is as bad or worſe than
' Death, may properly enough be call'd
' by that Name ; And for this Reaſon the

---

* Ita me Dii Deæq; omnes pejus perdant quam hodie periſe me ſentio, *&c.*

' Pu-

' Punishment of wicked Men after the
' Day of Judgment is in the Book of the
' *Revelation* so frequently and fitly call'd
' *the second Death**. And *the Lake of Fire*,
' into which the Wicked *shall be cast* to be
' tormented in it, is expresly call'd *the*
' *second Death*.

' But besides this, they that argue from
' the force of these Words, that the Punish-
' ment of wicked Men in the other World,
' shall be nothing else but an utter end of
' their Being, do necessarily fall into Two
' great Inconveniences.

' *First*, That hereby they 'exclude all
' positive Punishment and Torment of Sin-
' ners. For if *the second Death*, and to be
' destroy'd, and to *perish*, signifie nothing
' else but the *Annihilation* of Sinners, and
' an utter extinction of their Being; and
' if this be all the effect of that dreadful
' *Sentence* which shall be pass'd upon them
' at the *Day of Judgment*, then the *Fire of*
' *Hell* is quench'd all at once, and is only
' a frightful *Metaphor* without any mean-
' ing. But this is directly contrary to the
' tenor of *Scripture*, which doth so often
' describe the Punishment of wicked Men
' in Hell by positive Torments: And par-
' ticularly our Blessed *Saviour*, describing

---

* Rev. 20. 14.

' the

' the lamentable State of the damned in
' Hell, expresly says, that *there shall be*
' *weeping and wailing, and gnashing of Teeth.*
' Which cannot be, if Annihilation be all
' the meaning and effect of the Sentence
' of the Great Day.

' *Secondly,* Another Inconvenience of this
' Opinion is, that if *Annihilation* be all the
' Punishment of Sinners in the other World,
' then the Punishment of all Sinners must
' of necessity be equal, because there are
' no degrees of *Annihilation* or *not-being.*
' But this also is most directly contrary to
' *Scripture,* as I have already shown.

' I know very well that some who are
' of this Opinion do allow a very long and
' tedious Time of the most terrible and
' intolerable Torment of Sinners, and af-
' ter that they believe that there shall be
' an utter end of their Being.

' But then they must not argue this from
' the force of the Words before mentioned,
' because the plain Inference from thence
' is, that Annihilation is all the Punish-
' ment that wicked Men shall undergo in
' the next Life; and if that be not true,
' as I have plainly shewn that it is not, I
' do not see from what other Words or
' Expressions in *Scripture* they can find the
' least ground for this Opinion, that the
' Torment of wicked Men shall at last end
' in their *Annihilation.* And yet admit-

' ting

' ting all this, for which I think there is
' no ground at all in *Scripture,* I cannot
' fee what great Comfort Sinners can take
' in the thought of a tedious Time of ter-
' rible Torment, ending at laft in *Annihila-*
' *tion,* and the utter Extinction of their Be-
' ings.

We muft confefs that there is reafon to
tremble, tho' we only fuppofe that impenitent Sinners will be tormented by fome
terrible Punifhment, during the Time that
it fhall pleafe God, and whofe duration
will be unknown to them; they having no
end to expect of their Mifery, except it be
the entire Annihilation of their Being,
Thus without making the Punifhments to
be eternal, ftrictly fpeaking, a kind of
Torment may be fuppos'd, which is fufficient to fright and curb the Sinners. The
reafon that the Threats of the Gofpel do
not produce their due effect upon Men, is
not owing to the duration of the Torments
which the wicked are threaten'd with;
but altogether to this, that thofe Punifhments do not affect their Senfes, appearing
to them to be at a diftance. Prefent Plea-
fures blind them, and move their Paffions
fo violently, that the Ideas of a Futurity,
diftant as they imagine, do hardly affect
them.

Moreover, thofe that are for Pains
which muft end in an Annihilation, take
their

their Foundation for such an Opinion, partly from those Passages which mention positive Pains, as in all those Places where mention is made of a *Fire*, which will burn the wicked; and from thence they have their Idea of those terrible Punishments; and partly from those which speak of an *End*, as of *Death*, which according to them will put an end to that *Fire* by annihilating the Sinners, after they have been punish'd. But Archbishop TILLOTSON does justly object to them, that the Punishment of *Fire*, which is doubtless a positive Punishment, is nam'd the *second Death*, and consequently Death does not signify an Annihilation. Nevertheless, if any one disturb'd at the disproportion of eternal Pains with the Sins of Men, and for fear of offending the Divine Justice, shou'd rather choose to follow this Opinion, than that which is commonly receiv'd; I don't see why it shou'd be look'd upon as so great a Crime, and equal to the denying of the whole Gospel. They that accuse others so rashly, say enough to those Men that reflect upon it; and for those that do not, even the Eternity of the Punishment will not fright them, as Experience shews. At least, it is infinitely better for a Man to believe the Gospel, admitting of such a kind of Punishment, as to reject it wholly, because he cannot allow of eternal Punish-

ments

ments which the Gospel is said to teach.

' *Thirdly*, says Archbishop TILLOTSON,
' We may confider further, that the prima-
' ry end of all Threatnings is not Punish-
' ment, but the prevention of it. For God
' does not threaten that Men may sin and
' be punish'd, but that they may not sin,
' and fo may efcape the Punishment threat-
' ned. And therefore the higher the
' Threatning runs, fo much the more
' Mercy and Goodnefs there is in it; be-
' caufe it is fo much the more likely to hin-
' der Men from incurring the Penalty that
' is threatned.

' *Fourthly*, Let it be confidered likewife,
' that when it is fo very plain that God
' hath threatned eternal Mifery to impeni-
' tent Sinners, all the Prudence in the World
' obliges Men to believe that he is in good
' earneft, and will execute thefe Threat-
' nings upon them, if they will obftinate-
' ly ftand it out with him, and will not be
' brought to Repentance. And therefore
' in all Reafon we ought fo to demean our
' felves, and fo to perfwade others, as
' knowing the Terror of the Lord, and
' that they who wilfully break his Laws
' are in danger 'of eternal Death. To
' which I will add in the

' *Fifth* and laft Place, That if we fup-
' pofe that God did intend that his Threat-
' nings fhould have their effect to deter
         ' Men

' Men from the breach of his Laws, it
' cannot be imagin'd that in the fame Re-
' velation which declares thefe Threat-
' nings, any Intimation fhould be given
' of the Abatement or Non-execution of
' them. For by this God would have
' weakened his own Laws, and have ta-
' ken off the edge and terror of his Threat-
' nings; Becaufe a Threatning hath quite
' loft its Force, if we once come to be-
' lieve that it will not be executed: And
' confequently it would be a very impious
' Defign to go about to teach or perfwade
' any Thing to the contrary, and a be-
' traying Men into that Mifery which had
' it been firmly believ'd, might have been
' avoided.

' We are all bound to Preach, and you
' and I are all bound to believe the Terrors
' of the Lord. Not fo, as faucily to de-
' termine and pronounce what God muft
' do in this cafe; for after all, He may do
' what he will, as I have clearly fhewn:
' But what is fit for us to do, and what
' we have reafon to expect, if notwith-
' ftanding a plain and exprefs Threatning
' of the *Vengeance of eternal Fire*, we ftill
' go on *to treafure up to our felves Wrath a-*
' *gainft the Day of Wrath, and the Revelati-*
' *on of the Righteous Judgment of God*; and
' will defperately put it to the hazard, whe-
' ther, and how far, God will execute
                  ' his

' his Threatnings upon Sinners in another
' World.

'And therefore there is no need why
' we should be very solicitously concern'd
' for the Honour of God's Justice or Good-
' ness in this matter. Let us but take
' care to believe and avoid the Threatnings
' of God; and then how terrible soever
' they are, no harm can come to us. And
' as for God, let us not doubt but that he
' will take care of his own Honour; and
' that he, *who is Holy in all his Ways, and*
' *Righteous in all his Works,* will do nothing
' that is repugnant to his eternal Good-
' ness and Righteousness; and that he will
' certainly so manage Things at the Judg-
' ment of the Great Day, as *to be justified*
' *in his Sayings, and to be righteous when we*
' *are judged.* For notwithstanding his
' Threatnings, he hath reserved Power e-
' nough in his own Hands to do right to
' all his Perfections: So that we may rest
' assur'd that he will *judge the World in*
' *Righteousness*; and if it be any wise in-
' consistent either with Righteousness or
' Goodness, which he knows much better
' than we do, to make Sinners miserable
' for ever, that He will not do it; nor is
' it credible, that he would threaten Sin-
' ners with a Punishment which he could
' not execute upon them.
'

These

These Reflections of Archbishop TIL-
LOTSON's are, no doubt, full of good Sense
and Piety, and that Counsel may be follow'd which he very prudently gives.
Yet some People have censur'd this Place
in his Sermon, accusing him of having
spoken very imprudently. If God, say
those Men, has not given us any Expression in Holy Scripture, from which we may
imagine that he will not put his Threats
in Execution, left it should destroy the Effects of them; why does Archbishop TIL-
LOTSON in this Place insinuate, that perhaps God will not put them in Execution?
It is a great Imprudence to reveal what
God has been pleas'd to hide, and as it
were to betray his Secret. He should have
kept that Knowledge to himself (if he
thought he knew it) and not make it
known to those who might make an ill Use
of it.

But this is only Cavilling; for what he
has said can have no ill Effect; since in the
main, they that might make an ill Use of
such a Thought, must remember, that
Archbishop TILLOTSON only speaks doubt-
fully of it, that he was not infallible, and
that they shall not at all be more excusable
for having follow'd his Opinion, in case
that he was mistaken. If God has not ti-
ed his Hands by his Threats, much less
will he be oblig'd to act according to the

D   Con-

Conjectures of Divines. Thus we should
think and always act with the greatest
Caution to avoid the Effect of his Threats,
whatever it be. Nevertheless, we must
do Justice to this excellent Archbishop, and
observe, on the other hand, that there are
some Cases where it is well to discover
what in other Cases it would be proper to
conceal. If there were no Objections to be
made against the Eternity of the Torments,
it would not be well to meddle with that
Question; but since we know that there
are some Men who attack the Gospel on
that side, and pretend to shew that the
Doctrine of it is not confistent with it
felf; becaufe, as they fay, it affirms God
to be juft and good, and at the fame time
teaches that he punifhes Sin in a manner
that is not agreeable to his Juftice or Goodnefs. We are oblig'd to bring back fuch
Men, and to hinder their Reafonings from
being prejudicial to others, and encouraging them to Libertinifm. Therefore, to
prevent this Evil, and extirpate it juft as it
is taking Root, by putting an End to all
Difpute about it, we are oblig'd to declare,
That if any one can't perfwade himfelf that
eternal Torments are juft, he had better
look upon what the Gofpel fays of them as
Threats, or *Comminatory Punifhments* (as
the Expreffion is) than to reject the whole
Gofpel upon that Account. It is better in
fuch

ſuch a Caſe to be an *Origeniſt* than an Un-
believer ; that is, to disbelieve the Eternity of the Torments out of regard to God's
Juſtice and Goodneſs, and obey the Goſpel
in every thing elſe ; than wholly to reject
Revelation, imagining that it contains
ſomething contrary to the Idea which it ſelf
gives us of God, and which is conformable to the Light of Nature. Mr. *Camphuyſe*,
a Perſon famous in *Holland* upon account
of ſeveral Pieces of Poetry, has publickly
declared, that he had been tempted to reject the Chriſtian Religion altogether,
whilſt he believed that it taught the Eternity of Torments ; and that he never overcame thoſe Temptations, till he found that
the Threats of the Goſpel might be taken
in another Senſe. It was for promoting
the Salvation of ſuch doubting Men, that
Archbiſhop TILLOTSON ſpoke as he did.

Saint JEROM, at the end of his Commen-
tary upon *Iſaiah*, after quoting ſome Paſſa-
ges by which ORIGEN pretended to prove,
that the Puniſhments of the next Life would
not be eternal, expreſſes himſelf thus :
* ' They ſay all this, hoping to ſhew,
' that after the Puniſhments and Torments,
' Refreſhments will come, which muſt
' now be conceal'd from thoſe that can be
' acted upon by Fear, that the Dread of

---

* *Pag.* 514. *T.* 3. *Ed. Bened.*

' the

‘ the Punishment may keep them from
‘ sinning. We must leave this to the
‘ Knowledge of God alone, whose Punish-
‘ ments, as well as Mercies, are settled ;
‘ who knows whom, which way, and how
‘ long, he designs to punish. Let us only
‘ say what becomes human Frailty ; *O*
‘ *Lord, rebuke me not in thine Indignation ;*
‘ *neither chasten me in thy Displeasure. Quæ*
omnia replicant adseverare cupientes post cru-
ciatus & tormenta, futura refrigeria, quæ
nunc abscondenda sunt ab his quibus timor uti-
lis est ; ut dum supplicia reformidant, peccare
desistant. Quod nos Dei solius debemus sci-
entiæ derelinquere ; cujus non solùm miseri-
cordiæ, sed & tormenta in pondere sunt, &
novit quem, quomodo, aut quamdiu debeat
judicare. Solumque dicamus quod humanæ
convenit fragilitati : Domine, ne in furore
tuo arguas me, neque in ira tua corripias
me. This is much after Archbishop TIL-
LOTSON's manner. The Fear of eternal
Punishments, when it induces Men to o-
bey the Gospel, cannot but be useful (according to him) although it should be ill-
grounded ; and it would not be well to deliver from that Fear those on whom it
produces so good an effect.

But on the other hand, when we have
such Men to deal with as rebel against the
Gospel, upon account of the eternal Torments, and endeavour to seduce others
from

from believing it; it is better to let them believe the Punishments finite, than to throw them wholly off of the Christian Religion, or give them an Advantage to strive against it. St. JEROM himself was moderate in that case, as it appears by his Words following: ‘ As we believe that there are ‘ eternal Torments for the Devils, for all ‘ those that deny the Being of God, and ‘ for all the Impious, which say in their ‘ Hearts, *There is no God* ; so we believe ‘ that the Sentence of the Judge is softned ‘ and mix’d with Clemency towards those ‘ Sinners and impious Men which yet have ‘ been Christians, and whose Works must ‘ be prov’d and purg’d by Fire. *Et sicut Diaboli & omnium negatorum, atque impiorum, qui dixerunt in corde suo, non est Deus; credimus æterna tormenta: sic peccatorum atque impiorum, & tamen Christianorum, quorum opera in igne probanda sunt atque purganda, moderatam arbitramur & mistam clementiæ sententiam judicis.* Other Fathers have follow’d the same Notions, as may be seen in Mr. HUET’s *Origeniana,* Book 2. Quest. 11.

5. They who are of that Opinion, at least in some respects, believe that God may have threatned in such a manner, not only to awe Men by Fear, as a Father often threatens his Children with what he does not mean to do ; but because there being

D 3　　　　infinite

infinite kinds of Sinners and of Sins, there is no limited Term for all in common, and it is even a great Part of the Punishment that there is no positive Promise that it will have an End, or Knowledge of the Time when that End will be. This last will be wholly conceal'd, and the first is only a Consequence drawn from the Mercy and Justice of God, which are only known to himself. God will condemn the Impenitent to certain Pains without letting them know what he designs to do: As among Men, Criminals are publickly condemn'd to the Death which they have deserved, tho' there is an Order for their Pardon which they are not to be made acquainted with till the Moment that they expect to die. It might after the same manner happen (according to those whose Opinion I am explaining) that God would condemn to Pains *unlimited* as to their Duration, such Men as his Mercy would afterwards release at different times, after they had suffer'd as much as his Justice would require. The Holy Scripture would have call'd *Eternal*, such Punishments as are to be of an unlimited Duration in respect of the Creatures, and whose End is only known of God; which is the proper Meaning of the *Hebrew* Word עולם which is exprefs'd by the *Greek* Word αἰὼν, which signifies such a Time.

Supposing

Suppofing the Cafe to ftand thus, as indeed it may ; the Thought of fuch Punifhments is dreadful enough to caufe the moft
hardened to tremble; if they expect and
confider any fuch thing. As for thofe that
are altogether Unbelievers, they are no
more afraid of the Eternal Punifhments
which they don't believe, than of Limited
ones.

This Notion was made ufe of in the 1ft
Tome of the *Parrhafiana*, to endeavour to
bring back thofe whom the Objections of
Mr. BAYLE's *Manichæi*, (for I don't look
upon their Opinion as his) might have
ftartled, or diffwaded from the Belief of
Chriftianity. For indeed if the Holy
Scripture fhould reprefent God to us in a
manner different from the Idea which his
Works give us of him, as the Objections
Manichæi fuppofe; or if it fhould reprefent
God as an hurtful Being, and an Enemy
to Virtue, it cou'd not be a Divine Revelation. It would not be Piety but Folly,
to believe a Book to be from God which
fhould affirm any fuch thing, tho' the fame
Book fhould in other Places fay the contrary ; for it would be a Contradiction of
which the Spirit of God can no more be the
Author than he can be the Author of Evil.

Mr. BAYLE thought fit again to intro-
duce his *Manichæi*, and has anfwer'd for
them at full length to the Article concern-

D 4

ing

ing ORIGEN, in the fecond Edition
of his Dictionary. I fhall not undertake to confute them here in fo prolix a
manner, wanting Time, and not thinking
it neceffary. They who have that Dictionary may there read the Replies of the *Manichæi*; and I will fuppofe them known. I
believe Mr. BAYLE will not think me in
the wrong for defending the Chriftian Religion, the Truth of which I believe, and
for which I would lay down my Life, if
God fhould call me to it; when at the
fame time he thinks it allowable to furnifh
with Arms thofe which he thinks to be in
an Error, and for whom I don't fuppofe
that he would lofe the fmalleft Advantage.
If I have any fharp Expreffions againft the
Manichæi, they cannot reflect upon him,
who according to all Appearance difap-
proves their Doctrine; but I look upon
all the Attempts made by the *Manichæi* a-
gainft Chriftianity, as levell'd at me who
profefs it, and am perfwaded that nothing
can be found in the Chriftian Religion which
is contrary to Reafon. If it be ask'd why I
have not anfwer'd fooner, I fay that I did not
imagine that any body could have been led
afide by fuch Replies; but fince I underftand that fome People are puzzl'd with
them, I was willing to take Notice of 'em
in a few Words, to fhew that they are no
way terrible to me. It were to be wifh'd,

as

as I faid in the 6th *Tome*, that the *Mani-chei* wou'd eftablifh fome Principles, that one might be able to difpute with them. But I was willing to anfwer here directly, leaft what I then objected fhou'd be look'd upon as a Trick to fhift off the Difpute.

I fhall ftill reafon upon the Principles of the *Origenift*, which was introduc'd in the *Parrhafiana*; not to exact too much of the *Manichei*, or of thofe which like their Re-plies. It is better, as I faid before, to give them up fomething, and bring them over to the Gofpel; than to keep them at a diftance by requiring more of them than they wou'd be willing to grant. Mr. BAYLE's *Manichei* have in fome meafure been affected with it, fince they confefs that the *Origenift* of the *Parrhafiana*, by making eternal Happinefs fucceed the eter-nal Torments which the damned are to fuffer, *has taken off the greateft Difficulty of the* Manichei; *namely, the Eternity of the Moral and of the Phyfical Pains of Hell.* Mr. BAYLE indeed quotes a Jefuit, who fays fomething concerning the Opinion of ORIGEN, which does agree with all that the *Origenift* fays. We know that; but thought it as allowable for us to put what Words we pleas'd in the Mouth of the *Origenift*; as it was for Mr. BAYLE to make his *Manichei* fpeak after what man-ner he thought fit.

Firft,

First, The *Manichai* say that the Goodnefs of God, which, as we conceive it, ought to be an *Ideal Goodnefs*, that is, without any mixture of Ill-will, ought not to fuffer him to make us buy eternal Happinefs, with the fuffering of the leaft Pain, but he ought to do us Good without the leaft mixture of Evil. To this I anfwer, *Firft*, That God having made an infinite number of Creatures, of different Degrees of Perfection, to fhew his Power an infinite number of Ways; he has form'd Man, who in his Order is neither one of the moft perfect, nor one of the moft imperfect. *Secondly*, It cannot be doubted, but that the Divine Bounty can beftow more or lefs upon a Creature, according to his Pleafure: So that a Creature has no reafon to complain, becaufe God, who owed him nothing, has given him no more. *Thirdly*, God has not created the Mind of Man fo perfect, as to enable him never to wander from his Duty, or from the Rules which Reafon and Revelation prefcrib'd him to become acceptable to him, and happy even upon Earth; neither has he given him a Body fo ftrong, as not to be liable to feveral Inconveniences; but he has given him the Means of being happy, if he will but obferve the Rules prefcrib'd him, being oblig'd by no unconquerable Neceffity to violate them.

I

I affirm that there is nothing in this, that can give Men any reason to conceive any disadvantageous Notions of the Goodness of God. For the Goodness of God, however infinite in it self, is not oblig'd to communicate it self to every one of his Creatures, in the fulleft manner possible. If the Creator's Bounty is not free, nothing in the World can be so ; for by what Contract is the Creator oblig'd to give a Creature (which he designs to draw out of nothing) all that he can possibly bestow ? There can certainly be no such Contract, neither is there any Thing in his Nature to oblige him to be so communicative to every Creature, as to be unable to bestow any more upon it after having created it. If this was true, God must have made but one sort of Creatures, whereby this Liberality must have been so wholly exhausted, as to make him uncapable of bestowing any Thing more. Otherwise these Creatures might, according to the *Manichaan* Objection, say, that his *ideal* Goodness does not appear in his Works, and that they are not all equally well treated, nor with the same Liberality. From this also would follow a downright Absurdity, namely, that God's Creatures wou'd be as perfect as himself; that is, wou'd have infinite Perfections, which is impossible ; because otherwise it might still be said that God

might

might have given them infinite Degrees of Perfection, which he has not given them ; and consequently that his Goodnefs appears in them only limitted, and only capable of limitted Effects. After this rate God muft make as many Gods as Creatures, (which is a Contradiction) otherwife his *ideal* Goodnefs wou'd not appear.

What then muft be faid in this Cafe? That the Goodnefs of God is in it felf infinite, but that each Creature is finite, and therefore uncapable of exhaufting that Bounty. But the Infinity of God's Goodnefs appears, from the infinite number of Objects to which it is more or lefs extended, and that after an infinite number of Ways, efpecially as it beftows eternal Felicity on an infinite number of intelligent Creatures. After this manner alfo does the Almighty Power of God appear in the Univerfe ; not that God has made it either wholly, or in its Parts as perfect as himfelf, which wou'd imply a Contradiction ; but it fhews it felf in the vaft number of its Effects of all Kinds, whether known to us, or unknown to us, but perceiv'd by other intelligent Beings.

Secondly, Man's Imperfection has been the Reafon that he has made an ill ufe of his Liberty, and err'd from his Duty ; and this has brought upon him all the Evils which happen to him in this Life, and in
the

the next; from which God wou'd preserve him if he shou'd continue in Innocence. This is an Effect of the Liberty which he was created with. Had he made a good use of his Liberty, he might have procur'd himself the Favour of Heaven, and a Thousand Blessings which are the Consequence of it; but it has happen'd otherwise.

Here our *Manichæi* reply, that this Liberty is a fatal Gift, and that if Man was created by a good Being, he wou'd not have bestow'd on him such a Talent as he might have made an ill use of, in a manner destructive to himself; and which, according to us, God knew that he wou'd make an ill use of. They use all their Rhetoric to aggravate the Evil which this Gift has brought upon Mankind; and which they might have avoided, if he that made them, had created them of such a Nature that they cou'd not err from their Duty.

But all these Arguments against the Creator's Goodness, will vanish, if we consider well what I have before observ'd, and what the *Origenist* of the *Parrhasians* said upon that Subject. The Liberty of doing Ill is an Imperfection in such a fickle Creature as Man, if we compare him with Creatures of a more exalted Nature, which may be exempt from it; and the Divine Goodness does not tax him with it as a Crime. It only condemns him for the ill
Use

Use which he makes of it, because it is in his Power to make a good Use of it. And even to prevent that ill Use, and lead Man to Happiness, God has in the Gospel propos'd to him eternal Rewards, and *unlimited* Punishments. It is in Man's own Power to avoid these Punishments, and obtain the Rewards.

But then, say they, God knew what wou'd happen. It is true, certainly God was not mistaken in his Design, he did not intend to create Angels uncapable of Sinning, when he made Man; but before we go on, we must observe, that if the Divine Goodness has made Man liable to fall, it has also given him the greatest Motives possible to prevent his Fall. If he has been in danger of bringing Torments upon himself, he has also had the Power to avoid them; and not only so, but even to obtain eternal Happiness, which God was not oblig'd to give him. This being observ'd, I say, that God was not oblig'd to prevent by his Almighty Power, the Evil which he foresaw wou'd happen, thro' Man's own fault; because that Evil which is so much talk'd of, and against which some endeavour to enflame the vulgar and weak Minds, is but of a small Duration in it self, and in all its Consequences, and can no ways break the Order of the Universe; because God can take it off in a mo-

moment, and will at laft do it for all Eternity, according to the Opinion of the *Origeniff.*

But, why muft Men go through Evil, before they can feel all the Effects of the Divine Goodnefs? I have already anfwer'd, that this is a Confequence of Man's imperfect Nature; which cou'd not have that Degree of Imperfection which it has, without being liable to what has happen'd. Either we muft fay, that God cou'd make nothing imperfect, compar'd with himfelf, which is abfurd, as I have fhewn; or we muft grant that he made Beings that want fomething, and which have been expos'd to the Inconveniencies which were the refult of that Want; but that God may remove thofe Inconveniencies when he pleafes, and after what manner he pleafes.

As for Example, God cannot make Creatures without beginning, becaufe to be created, and to have no beginning are contradictory Propofitions. Neverthelefs, this Confequence may be drawn from it, *viz.* That God has been an infinite fpace of Time, or a Time without beginning, without fhewing his Goodnefs. Yet (I dare fay) there is not any one fo void of Senfe as to complain becaufe God has not from all Eternity made him fenfible of his Bleffings; as being a Thing which implies a Contradiction. But God manifefts his

Good-

Goodnefs to intelligent Creatures, during another kind of Eternity of which they are capable, that is, for a Duration without end. Thus it is that God remedies the Inconveniency which arifes from the Nature of the Creature, which, how perfect foever it be in its Kind, muft have had a Beginning. So in refpect of a Creature of a changeable Nature, and which changes for the worfe, becaufe God has left it its Liberty; he afterwards brings a Remedy for that Misfortune, in fuch a wonderful manner, as the Creature is bound for ever to give him Thanks, and not to quarrel with the Almighty, for not having been made of a more exalted Nature, after fuch an unworthy manner as the *Manichei* do.

Thirdly, If God had made Men of fuch a Nature, as not only to be liable to fall; but alfo never to rife again when once he was fallen, and God had forefeen that he wou'd actually fall and fo never rife again upon any Account whatever; it might be faid that God had created him for that Fall and its Confequences. But God, who has forefeen that Man wou'd fall, does not damn him for that; but becaufe being able to rife again, he rifes not; that is, becaufe he freely retains his evil Habits till the end of his Life. This is a ftep of Mercy already very confiderable. *Firft,* Becaufe no one is

caft

caſt into the Torments of the Impenitents, but by his own fault. *Secondly,* Becauſe a great many lay hold of this Goodneſs of God, and riſing from their Sins, form Virtuous Habits, by which they avoid the Pains of the next Life, and beforehand taſte a great deal of Calm and Sweetneſs even in this.

As for the others, on whom God inflicts Puniſhments after Death, and who by their folly bring Evil upon themſelves, and upon each other during this Life: After God has puniſh'd them according to his Juſtice, he will (if we believe the *Origeniſt*) transfer them to a State of eternal Felicity. Thus it is that God ſhews an infinite Mercy; and as to the impenitent, there will not be any one of them, but what will accuſe himſelf of all the Evil that he has ſuffer'd, and at laſt give God Thanks for ever. *Firſt,* That God had created them ſuch as to be able to attain eternal Happineſs. *Secondly,* Becauſe tho' they had made ſuch an ill Uſe of their Liberty, yet notwithſtanding all that, God has not for ever excluded them from Happineſs, but has been willing (after the Sinners have juſtly ſuffer'd the Puniſhment due to their Impenitence) to admit them to that Happineſs which they had not purſued tho' God had ſhew'd them the Way. They will not any more remember either the Pains of this Life, or the Pains of the other, except it be to thank God that they are deli-

ver'd

ver'd from them, and to admire the more his Mercy and Goodnefs. For indeed we do not know how far God may carry the Torments, according to the rigor of his Juftice; neither can we fay that he will not annihilate the Impenitent after they have endured Hell Torments. Abfolutely fpeaking, God can take away from the Creature all that he has given it; and if he does not do it (efpecially when an ill Ufe has been made of his Gifts) he thereby fhews his Mercy. The Impenitent therefore will always have great Occafion to thank God, and accufe themfelves; inftead of cenfuring him, as Mr. BAYLE's *Manichæi* do. Who doubts but that it is infinitely more advantageous to have been created, tho' liable to fome Inconveniencies, than never to have been created at all? Who does not fee the Divine Goodnefs fhine in this, in a manner worthy of it felf?

Fourthly, But Mr. BAYLE's *Manichæi* make this further Objection, *viz.* that if it be faid that the Duration of the Evils which Man fuffers here, and in the other Life, is nothing, when compar'd with Eternity, it will give Occafion to this unphilofophical Reafoning, namely, that according to this Principle an Hundred Thoufand Millions of Ages, and any other finite Duration, during which the Creatures fhou'd fuffer, muft be look'd upon as nothing,

when

when compar'd with Eternity. I answer,
First, That it is true that a past Duration,
how long foever it has been, is nothing in
respect of Eternity, if it has no evil
Consequence, of everlasting Duration.
This cannot be doubted of, if we are but
capable of Reasoning; for there is no
Comparison between Finite and Infinite,
and a Philosopher who shou'd argue otherwise deserves to be sent to School again.
Thus when a Creature has thro' its own
fault suffer'd any determinate Time, when
it might have avoided, there will be no
comparison between the Severity and the
Goodness of God. This is a Thing of Ma-
thematical Evidence, not to be disputed
by any one that knows how to think. But,
Secondly, To satisfy even such Arguers, an
Origenist, who rightly understands his own
Principles, will answer, that he does not
define the Duration of the Torments, but
that they will be longer or shorter, as Justice shall require. According to the same
Principles, the Duration of the Torments
will be shorter as the Torments are sharp-
er; and there will be as much Variety in
the Punishments, as there was in the Sins.
But if it shou'd be replied, that the Duration of the Torments will be long in respect
to the Life of the Impenitent, and to the
Time of the evil Consequences of their
misbehaviour, an *Origenist* need not fear

that

that such a Notion shou'd be prov'd absurd, or contrary to the Holy Scripture. Because what is objected against him concerning Torments that are to last several Ages does no way confute his Assertions; for he does not believe that they will last so long, tho' he cannot determine their Duration. It can't be alledg'd against him, that a long or a short Duration differ only comparatively; since the Duration of the Pains must be proportion'd to the Sins and to all their Circumstances.

Fifthly, Mr. BAYLE's *Manichæi* say that all the Advantage which the *Origenists* seem to have in this Dispute, is owing to the falsities which are proper to them; as on the one Hand, giving a great extent to the Power of the Free-Will; and on the other, substituting eternal Happiness instead of the eternal Torments, which they suppress. But the *Origenists* will answer the *Manichæi*, that they are very bold to call that Falshood which ORIGEN has taught concerning Free-Will, when themselves have been condemn'd, not only by all the rest of Mankind, who acknowledge Free-Will; but also by the whole Christian Church, which has constantly detested the Doctrine of MANES, concerning Free-Will, which he deny'd. It is not ORIGEN alone who has attack'd this Opinion of MANES; but all who have spoken of this Heretick, and have detested
ed

ed his Doctrine, whether Eastern or Weſtern Writers; eſpecially before the Diſputes with the *Pelagians.* The *Origeniſts* wou'd alſo alledge, that it is falſe to ſay that it may be concluded from the Terms of Holy Scripture, that the Torments will be eternal; and there is no need of dwelling any more upon that Topic after what has been ſaid. I do not believe that the Objections of the *Manichæi* againſt the Goodneſs of God can be call'd *unexceptionable Truths*; or that the Anſwers of the *Origeniſts* in Defence of the Divine Goodneſs can be term'd *falſities*; ſince, Philoſophically ſpeaking, the Opinions of the latter have a Foundation infinitely ſtronger, againſt which the *Manichæi* can make no reaſonable Objection.

Sixthly, Nothing then can be more abſurd, than wholly to deny Hell Torments, to defend the Divine Goodneſs. An *Origeniſt*, by ſuppoſing them Finite, eaſily removes all Difficulties. He finds in God the following Tokens of Goodneſs, and ſuch a Goodneſs as muſt truly be infinite. Namely, *Firſt*, That God has created Men to be kind to them, out of pure Goodneſs; for having no Being we had not done any Thing which cou'd bring on us the Effects of his Kindneſs. *Secondly,* He has given them a Thouſand excellent Qualities, as appears by the Invention of Arts and Scien-

E 3

ces,

ces, both Speculative and Practical. *Thirdly,* He has encompass'd them with a numberless quantity of sensible Benefits or Blessings that affect their Senses, which are enjoy'd with a great deal of Pleasure, and tend much to their Advantage, if they are used moderately: And as for Life, all Men love it, except a few melancholly People. *Fourthly,* He has shewn them, by Reason and Revelation, the Things which were necessary to be known in order to their obtaining Happiness (by their Obedience to him) both in this Life and after Death. *Fifthly,* The Commands which he has laid on them, are of such a Nature, that they cannot but be happy in observing them; since they all promote the good of Human Nature, and all Men reap an Advantage from them; for they can bestow nothing on the Almighty, who has no more need of them after once he has created them, than he had in the Duration without end, which preceeded the Creation of the World. *Sixthly,* God's Commands are easy to be observ'd, if we will conform our selves to right Reason; and nothing can make them difficult but a contrary Habit. *Seventhly,* Such an Habit may be overcome, and if we fall, God is not implacable; he will be satisfied if we do but rise again. *Eighthly,* He immediately gives eternal Happiness to those that have repented, and punishes the

Im-

Impenitent with moderate Torments, before he lets them enter in Possession of that said eternal Happiness, which shows, that has created Man with a design to make him Happy; which if Man has not been at first, is only thro' his own fault.

Nothing can be objected against this but the Inconveniences, which are annex'd to an intelligent Nature which is liable to change, and which God was not willing to prevent; because he look'd upon them as nothing in Comparison of the Good which he has resolv'd to bless Mankind with. But then (say the Disciples of MAMES) must not a Mother, who foresees that her Daughter will yield to the Temptations of a debauch'd Man, make haste and hinder her, if she has a value for her Daughter, and for Chastity? Can she her self be reckon'd honest, if she does not prevent it? We say nothing here of the indecency of comparing Divine Providence with a Woman that prostitutes her Daughter, tho' our Respect for God Almighty ought hardly to bear with such a way of speaking. In a Word, the *Manichei* are abominable Heretics, Enemies of the Holy Scripture and the Gospel, in using such Expressions; and surely, the Gentleman that pleads for them cannot be of their Opinion. But to the foremention'd Objection we answer, that such a Mother, ought, as much as in

her

her lies, to prevent the Evil which she fears. *First*, Because she is so commanded in the Gospel. *Secondly*, Because when the Mischief is done she can no way remedy it, or prevent its evil Consequences. *Thirdly*, Because the Evil which such a Woman suffers to be committed, and its Consequences, are in respect to her self as well as her Daughter, great and considerable. But God, who is our Creator and Lawgiver, may permit a Work which he has made fickle, to be (as it were) out of Order; because such an Inconvenience is scarce any Thing in respect to him, and he can easily remedy it as soon as he shall think fit. This is what the *Origenist* has shewn in his *Parrhasiana*; where with a handful of Dust, *pulveris exigui jactu*, he has laid a swarm of Difficulties, which were in a pompous manner brought in concerning the Disorder that we see in the World, whose End we cannot yet any way foresee.

Besides, what has been said may as well be applied to Moral as to Physical Evil, to the Vices, as to the Sufferings of Men; and we need not make any distincter Application of it to these Two Kinds of Disorders.

Neither shall I take up any Time to shew, that if the Holy Scripture taught us any Thing unworthy of God, or implied

plied

plied contradictory Notions, it cou'd not
be of Divine Infpiration, or chain our
Faith. The Thing is felf-evident; therefore I enlarge no more upon this Head,
leaving the Reader to think the reft; becaufe I wou'd not appear to make the *Ori-*
geniſt triumph, leaft odious Confequences
fhou'd be drawn from it.

Laſtly, If any one fhou'd take it ill that
I reafon upon the Principles of an *Origeniſt,*
tho' I am not altogether of ORIGEN's O-
pinion; he muft confider, that I did not
begin, *Firſt,* to cover my felf with a bor-
row'd Name; I was only willing by this
to imitate Mr. BAYLE, who has taken upon him to perfonate the *Manichæi.* Se-
condly, They that have nicely examin'd
ORIGEN's Opinion, have acknowledg'd,
that bating fome *Platonic* Whimfies, which
may be blotted out of his Syftem without
overthrowing it; (fuch as the Præ-exi-
ftence of Souls, the Revolutions of all
Things in fettled Periods, and other fuch
Notions) the reft has been generally receiv'd and efteem'd by all the Eaft; till
THEOPHILUS of *Alexandria,* and other hot
Men of his Time, caus'd him to be condemn'd, rather to overthrow fuch Men as
they hated, than out of regard to Truth.
Befides, ORIGEN has always been look'd
upon as a Member of the Chriftian Church,
in which alfo he died; after he had been

a Confeffor, during the Perfecution of *Decius* ; and had fhewn a great deal of Conftancy, and appear'd very willing to fuffer Martyrdom. A great many have formerly, and of late Years, written in his Defence, whofe Books any one may confult. And then what ORIGEN has advanc'd concerning the end of Hell Torments, was but what he thought he found in the Holy Scripture, which he endeavour'd to explain after the beft manner that he cou'd He only argued for its Authority, but the *Manichæi* directly againft it.

But after fo long a Digreffion, let us hearken anew to Archbifhop TILLOTSON, who will fhew us what ufe we ought to make of the manner in which the Holy Scripture has exprefs'd the Pains of the next Life.

' Therefore Sinners, *fays he*, ought always to be afraid of it, and reckon upon it ; and always to remember, that there is great Goodnefs and Mercy in the feverity of God's Threatnings; and that nothing will more juftify the Infliction of eternal Torments, than the foolifh Prefumption of Sinners in venturing upon them, notwithftanding fuch plain and terrible Threatnings.

' This I am fure, is a good Argument to all of us, to *work out our Salvation with fear and trembling* ; and with all poffible
' care

' care to endeavour the prevention of that
' Misery which is so terribly severe, that
' at present we can hardly tell how to re-
' concile it with the Justice and Goodness
' of God.

' This God heartily desires we would
' do; and hath solemnly sworn, that *he*
' *hath no Pleasure in the Death of the wicked,*
' *but rather that he should turn from his wiç-*
' *kedness and live.* So that here is all ima-
' ginable care taken to prevent our miscar-
' riage, and all the Assurance that the God
' of Truth can give us of his unwillingness
' to bring this Misery upon us. And both
' these, I'm sure, are Arguments of great
' Goodness. For what can Goodness do
' more, than to warn us of this Misery,
' and earnestly perswade us to prevent it;
' and to threaten us so very terribly on pur-
' pose to deter us from so great a danger?

' And if this will not prevail with us,
' but we will go still on to *despise the Riches*
' *of God's goodness, and long-suffering, and*
' *forbearance;* what in Reason remains for
' us, *but a fearful looking for of Judgment,*
' *and fiery Indignation to consume us?* And
' what almost can Justice, or even Good-
' ness it self do less, than to inflict that Pu-
' nishment upon us, which with Eyes open
' we would wilfully run upon; and which
' no Warning, no Perswasion, no Impor-
' tunity could prevail with us to avoid?
' And

'And when, as the *Apostle* says, *knowing
'the Judgment of God, that they which com-
'mit such Things are worthy of Death*; yet
'for all that we would venture to com-
'mit them.

'And therefore, whatever we suffer,
'we do but inherit our own Choice, and
'have no reason to complain of God, who
'hath set before us Life and Death, eter-
'nal Happiness and Misery, and hath left
'us to be the Carvers of our own Fortune:
'And if, after all this, we will obstinate-
'ly refuse this Happiness, and wilfully
'run upon this Misery, *Wo unto us! for we
'have rewarded Evil to our selves*:

'You see then, by all that hath been
'said upon this Argument, what we have
'all reason to expect, if we will still go on
'in our Sins, and will not be brought to
'Repentance. You have heard, what a
'terrible Punishment the just God had
'threatned to the Workers of Iniquity;
'And that in as plain Words as can be u-
'sed to express any Thing. *These*, that is,
'the Wicked, *shall go away into everlasting
'Punishment, but the Righteous into Life
'eternal.*

'Here are *Life* and *Death*, Happiness
'and Misery set before us. Not this frail
'and mortal Life, which is hardly worth
'the having, were it not in order to a bet-
'ter and happier Life; nor a temporal
'Death,

'Death, to get above the dread whereof
'should not methinks be difficult to us,
'were it not for the bitter and terrible
'Consequences of it: But an eternal Life,
'and an eternal Enjoyment of all Things
'which can render Life pleasant and hap-
'py; and a perpetual Death, which will
'for ever torment us, but never make an
'end of us.

'These God propounds to our choice:
'And if the confideration of them will not
'prevail with us to leave our Sins, and to
'reform our Lives, what will? Weightier
'Motives cannot be propos'd to the Un-
'derftanding of Man, *than everlafting Pu-*
'*nifhment,* and *Life eternal*; than the
'greateft and moft durable Happinefs,
'and the moft intolerable and lafting Mi-
'fery that human Nature is capable of.

'Now, confidering in what Terms the
'Threatnings of the Gofpel are exprefs'd,
'we have all the reafon in the World to
'believe that the Punifhment of Sinners in
'another World will be everlafting. How-
'ever, we cannot be certain of the con-
'trary, Time enough to prevent it; nor
'till we come there, and find it by Expe-
'rience how it is: And if it prove fo, it
'will then be too late either to prevent that
'terrible Doom, or to get it revers'd.

'Some comfort themfelves with the un-
'comfortable, and uncertain hope of being
'dif-

‘ difcharg'd out of Being, and reduc'd to
‘ their firſt Nothing; at leaſt, after the
‘ tedious and terrible ſuffering of the moſt
‘ grievous and exquiſite Torments for in-
‘ numerable Ages. And if this ſhould
‘ happen to be true; good God! how fee-
‘ ble, how cold a Comfort is this ? Where
‘ is the Reaſon and Underſtanding of Men,
‘ to make this their laſt Refuge and Hope;
‘ and to lean upon it as a Matter of mighty
‘ Conſolation, that they ſhall be miſerable
‘ beyond all imagination, and beyond all
‘ Patience, for God knows how many A-
‘ ges? *Have all the workers of Iniquity no*
‘ *Knowledge?* No right Senſe and Judge-
‘ ment of Things ? No conſiderationǀ and
‘ care of themſelves, no concernment for
‘ their own laſting Intereſt and Happineſs?
  ‘ *Origen,* I know not for what good Rea-
‘ ſon, is ſaid to have been of Opinion, That
‘ the Puniſhment of Devils and wicked Men,
‘ after the Day of Judgment, will continue
‘ but for a Thouſand Years; and that af-
‘ ter *that* Time, they ſhall all be finally
‘ ſaved. I can very hardly perſwade my
‘ ſelf, that ſo wiſe and learned a Man as
‘ *Origen* was, ſhould be poſitive in an Opi-
‘ nion for which there can be no certain
‘ ground in Reaſon, eſpeeially for the pun-
‘ ctual and preciſe Term of a thouſand
‘ Years; and for which there is no ground at
‘ all, that I know of from Divine Revelation.
                                          ‘ But

' But upon the whole Matter, however
' it be ; be it for a Thousand Years, or be
' it for a longer and unknown Term, or be
' it for ever, which is plainly threatned in
' the Gospel : I say, however it be, this is
' certain, that it is infinitely wiser to take
' care to avoid it, than to dispute it, and
' to run the final hazard of it. Put it
' which way we will, especially if we put
' it at the worst, as in all prudence we
' ought to do, it is by all possible means
' to be provided against : So terrible, so
' intolerable is the Thought, yea, the
' very least suspicion of being miserable for
' ever.

' And now give me leave to ask you, as
' St. *Paul* did King *Agrippa*, *Do you believe*
' *the Scriptures?* And I hope I may answer
' for you, my self, as he did for *Agrippa*,
' *I know you do believe them.* And in them
' these Things are clearly revealed, and
' are part of that *Creed* of which we make
' a solemn Profession every Day.

' And yet, when we consider how most
' Men live, is it credible that they do firm-
' ly believe this plain Declaration of our
' *Saviour* and our *Judge*, That *the wicked*
' *shall go into everlasting Punishment, but*
' *the Righteous into Life eternal.*

' Or if they do in some sort believe it,
' is it credible that they do at all consider
' it seriously, and lay it to Heart? So that
'   ' if

' if we have a mind to reconcile our Be-
' lief with our Actions, we must either al-
' ter our *Bible* and our *Creed,* or we must
' change our Lives.

' Let us then *confider, and fhew our felves*
' *Men.* And if we do fo, can any Man to
' pleafe himfelf for a little while be con-
' tented to be punifhed for ever ; and for
' the fhadow of a fhort and imperfect Hap-
' pinefs in this Life, be willing to run the
' hazard of being really and eternally Mi-
' ferable in the next World?

' Surely this Confideration alone, of the
' extreme and endlefs Mifery of impenitent
' Sinners in another World, if it were but
' well wrought into our Minds, would be
' fufficient to kill all the Temptations of
' this World, and to lay them dead at our
' Feet ; and to make us deaf to all the En-
' chantments of Sin and Vice : Becaufe
' they bid us fo infinitely to our Lofs, when
' they offer us the enjoyment of a fhort
' Pleafure, upon fo very hard and unequal
' a Condition, as that of being miferable
' for ever.

' The eternal Rewards and Punifhments
' of another Life, which are the great San-
' ction and Security of God's Laws, one
' would think fhould be a fufficient weight
' to caft the Scales againft any Pleafure, or
' any Pain, that this World can tempt, or
' threaten us withal.

' And

'And yet, after all this, will we still
'go on to do wickedly, when *we know the*
'*Terrors of the Lord*, and that we must one
'Day answer all our bold Violations of
'his Law, and Contempts of his Authority,
'with the loss of our immortal Souls, and
'by *suffering the Vengeance of eternal Fire?*
    'What is it then that can give Men the
'*Heart* and *Courage*; but I recal that
'Word, because it is not true *Courage*,
'but *Fool-hardiness*, thus to out-brave the
'Judgment of God, and to set at nought
'the horrible and amazing Consideration
'of a miserable Eternity? How is it possi-
'ble that Men that are awake, and in
'their Wits, should have any ease in their
'Minds, or enjoy so much as one quiet
'Hour, whilst so great a danger hangs o-
'ver their Heads, and they have taken
'no tolerable care to prevent it? If we
'have any true and just Sense of this Dan-
'ger, we cannot fail to shew that we have
'it, by making haste to escape it, and by
'taking that care of our Souls, which is
'due to immortal Spirits that are made to
'be Happy or Miserable to all Eternity.
    Archbishop TILLOTSON goes on with
such Exhortations to the end of his Sermon. What I have quoted is sufficient to
shew such as have not read his Works,
how much they deserve that Praise which
they have met with.
G   The.

The ſafeſt and wiſeſt Way, as to the Torments of the next Life, is to believe that God will never do any Thing but what is agreeable to his Divine Attributes; and at the ſame Time to uſe all the care imaginable to avoid the Effects of his Threats; which (whatever it be) ſhall be the more terrible, the more it is deſpis'd. Nothing offends a Law-giver more, than to ſee that the greater his Threats are, the leſs they are regarded; and that inſtead of meeting with Obedience, they are cavill'd at. Then let ſuch as complain of God's Threats, be now ſilent, and ſtrive to obey him; it will be Time enough for them to complain when they have ſeen the Execution of them, if then they think them unjuſt. But let theſe Men beware, leſt they ſhou'd bring them upon their own Heads, by complaining before hand, of what they have not yet been made ſenſible of.

FINIS.

SOME

CORRECTIONS *of,*

AND

ADDITIONS *to,*

THE

L I F E

OF

Arch-Bishop TILLOTSON.

APPENDIX.

SOME

Corrections *of*, and Additions *to*, the LIFE of *Arch-Bishop* TIL-LOTSON.

Feb. 20, 17$\frac{16}{17}$.

Mr. CURLL,

AS I contributed the Materials at *Page* 10, 19, 20, 21, 36, 134, 135. in order to the Compiling the Life of that excellent Man, Arch-Bishop TILLOTSON, so I hope it may be of some Service to point out some Mistakes the Gentleman has made, who drew it up, in order to the correcting them.

It is said he was Curate to Bishop WILKINS at St. *Lawrence*'s, *before* the Re-storation, which can't be, for Dr. WILKINS was not Instituted to it till *April* 11. 1662.

Page 19.

H 2

upon

upon the Promotion of his immediate Predeceffor and Friend Dr. WARD to the Bifhoprick of *Exeter*. Neither can I find, that he was ever Curate to Dr. WILKINS, nor is it probable. He did not leave his Rectory of *Ketten*, where he refided, and which is worth near 200 *l.* ℣ *Annum*, till Dr. WILKINS had by his Intereft procured him to be made the *Tuefday* Lecturer there, and the Society of *Lincoln's-Inn* had chofen him Preacher there. See *Newcourt's* Parochial Hiftory of the Diocefe of *London*, Vol. 1. p. 387, 388.

Page 30. It is faid he was Dean of *Norwich*, which is another great Miftake, as you may fee in Sir THOMAS BROWNE's *Antiquities of the Cathedral Church of* NORWICH (a Book printed by your felf) where at *Page* 47. you have an exact Lift of the Deans of *Norwich*. He was Refidentiary of St. PAUL's in King CHARLES the Second's Time, as you may fee in *Newcourt*, Vol. 1. p. 147, 192. which was long before the Year 1689. He was made Refidentiary there by King CHARLES II. *Feb.* 14. 1677.

Page 48. He is called Dean of St. PAUL's, when he encourag'd Mr. GOUGE's *Welch Charity*, who died in 1681, and yet lived to fee the Books printed and difperfed according to his pious Defign.

Here

Here the Compiler seems to be a Stran- *Page 74,* ger to the Biſhop's Family, in miſtaking *& 138.* the Death of his only Child and *Daughter* for that of his *Son.* Mr. JANAWAY's Letter was writ to Mr. CHADWICK, who had married that Daughter, with whom he had only one Thouſand Pounds, the Biſhop ſaying it was a Gentlewoman's Fortune, and would not be prevailed with to give her more, tho' Mr. CHADWICK was a Gentleman of a good Eſtate and Family.

It is ſtrange, that no particular Enquiry has been made, to know what Poſterity the Biſhop left, which I think are Two Sons and a Daughter, his Grand-Children by his Daughter. The Daughter I perceive by Mr. NELSON's Will (the noted Non-juror) married one Mr. FOWLER, probably a Son of Biſhop FOWLER, or Grandſon.

Here that part of his excellent Prayer, *Page 97.* (which is in the 14th Vol. of his Sermons) ſhould have been inſerted, wherein, *he bleſſes God, that he was born of Honeſt and Religious Parents —— and that he had enabled him to return to them and their Children the Kindneſs he received from them, and to be ſtill a Father to them.*

I wonder very much that Mr. LESLEY *Page 120.* ſhould be made the Author of *ſome Diſcourſes upon* Dr. BURNET and Dr. TILLOTSON,

LOTSON, &c. when all the World knows they were written by Dr. HICKES, who never difowned them, and whom Bifhop BURNET pointed to fo often in his Anfwer to them, and almoft named him, befides the very great difference of the Stile from Mr. LESLEY's, and likenefs or famenefs rather with the Doctor's.

Page 138. Put *Daughter* in the room of *Son*, as was noted before.

It may be here added, that the Bifhop was buried near his dear Friend Bifhop WILKINS (no doubt) according to his Order and Defire; for that Bifhop WILKINS was buried under the North-Wall of the Chancel of the Church of St. *Lawrence*, as you may fee in *Newcourt*, Vol. 1. p. 388. and in *Wood's Athen. Oxon*, Vol. 2. p. 370.

Page 137. I forgot to obferve here, that it feems to have been proper to have given an Account of the Death of the Arch-Bifhop's Lady, Mrs. TILLOTSON, who departed this Life, as the publick Prints did fay, *Jan.* 20. 1704. and where fhe was buried, which I know not, but fuppofe by her Husband.

A Gentleman of *Hertfordfhire*, who was a Juftice of Peace in the late Reigns, and a violent Profecutor of the *Diffenters*, had got Dr. TILLOTSON's Picture in his
Par-

Parlour. The Dr. was drawn with his Gown on, and a Cloak upon one Shoulder, which he shew'd often to Strangers for their Diversion, and to expose and ridicule the Doctor, into whose Company and Conversation he afterwards accidentally fell, and was so pleased and charmed with it, and satisfied in his Character, that he declared his Grief for what he had done, and burnt the Picture.

Arch-Bishop TILLOTSON was fully satisfied long before he died, as he declared to an *eminent Clergyman* *, that his long projected Design of a COMPREHENSION was utterly *impracticable*, and that the *Dissenters* would never comply with any Abatements in Ceremonies, or other Terms of Conformity, nor any Thing less than the entire Overthrow of our present Church Polity and Service, and the hoisting their own new-fangled Scheme into the Place of it. And indeed Dr. CALAMY, who may be presumed to speak the Mind of the rest of his Party, tells the World very frankly, and with much Integrity, and without shuffling or prevaricating (which has been, and is but too

---

* *The Reverend Mr.* CHADWICK, *Rector of* Wormley *in* Hertfordshire, *who was very intimate with him.*

much

much used in this Cafe, when they are
preffed to declare how far they would
conform in order to their coming into the
Church) —— " *That in order to a Coali-*
" *tion we muſt part with our* EPISCOPACY
" *and* LITURGY, *and with all the* CERE-
" MONIES, *and in general with whatever*
" (they are pleafed to fay) *is not of Di-*
" *vine Inſtitution.*" See, Defence of *Mo-*
derate Non-conformity, Part III. p. 190.

And this is agreeable to the Refolutions
and Declarations of the *Non-Conformiſts* in
Queen ELIZABETH's Reign. See *Collier's*
Church Hiftory, *Vol.* 2. *p.* 586. and in
that of King CHARLES I. Biſhop HACKET's
Life of Arch-Biſhop WILLIAMS, *Part* 2.
p. 147.

F I N I S.

9 781120 897879